The Electronic Briefcase for Administrators

Tools and Templates

Susan Brooks-Young

International Society for Technology in Education

EUGENE, OREGON

The Electronic Briefcase for Administrators
TOOLS AND TEMPLATES

Susan Brooks-Young

Director of Publishing
Jean Marie Hall

Acquisitions Editors
Mathew Manweller
Scott Harter

Production Editor
Tracy Cozzens

Copy Editor
Nancy Olson

Book Design and Layout
Kim McGovern

Cover Design
Signe Landin

International Society for Technology in Education (ISTE)
480 Charnelton Street
Eugene, OR 97401-2626
Order Desk: 1.800.336.5191
Order Fax: 1.541.302.3778
Customer Service: orders@iste.org
Books and Courseware: books@iste.org
Permissions: permissions@iste.org
World Wide Web: www.iste.org

First Edition
ISBN 1-56484-183-9

About ISTE

The International Society for Technology in Education (ISTE) is a nonprofit professional organization with a worldwide membership of leaders in educational technology. We are dedicated to promoting appropriate uses of information technology to support and improve learning, teaching, and administration in PK–12 education and teacher education. As part of that mission, ISTE provides high-quality and timely information, services, and materials, such as this book.

The ISTE Publishing Department works with experienced educators to develop and produce classroom-tested books and courseware. We look for content that emphasizes the use of technology where it can make a difference—making the teacher's job easier; saving time; motivating students; helping students who have unique learning styles, abilities, or backgrounds; and creating learning environments that would be impossible without technology. We believe technology can improve the effectiveness of teaching while making learning exciting and fun.

Every manuscript and product we select for publication is peer reviewed and professionally edited. While we take pride in our publications, we also recognize the difficulties of maintaining quality while keeping on top of the latest technologies and research. Please let us know which products you would find helpful. We value your feedback on this book and other ISTE products. E-mail us at **books@iste.org**.

ISTE is home of the National Educational Technology Standards (NETS) Project, the National Educational Computing Conference (NECC), and the National Center for Preparing Tomorrow's Teachers to Use Technology (NCPT[3]). To learn more about NETS or request a print catalog, visit our Web site at **www.iste.org**, which provides:

- Current educational technology standards for PK–12 students, teachers, and administrators

- A bookstore with online ordering and membership discount options

- *Learning & Leading with Technology* magazine and the *Journal of Research on Technology in Education*

- *ISTE Update*, online membership newsletter

- Teacher resources

- Discussion groups

- Professional development services, including national conference information

- Research projects

- Member services

About the Author

Susan Brooks-Young has been involved in the field of instructional technology since 1979. She was one of the original users of technology in the district where she taught and has continued to explore ways in which technology can be used to facilitate student learning. She has worked as a computer mentor, technology trainer, and technology curriculum specialist. As a site administrator, she continued to place a high priority on technology and in 1993 founded Computer Using Educators' (CUE) Administrators Special Interest Group, which still serves as a network and resource for school administrators across the country and in Canada.

Prior to establishing her own consulting firm, Susan was a teacher, site administrator, and technology specialist at a county office of education in a career that spanned more than 23 years. She now spends her time working with school districts and regional centers exploring technology-related issues, developing curriculum, presenting workshops, teaching online courses, and writing articles for a variety of education journals.

Susan cochairs ISTE's Special Interest Group for Administrators. She authored the popular ISTE books *Making Technology Standards Work for You—A Guide for School Administrators* (2002) and *101 Best Web Sites for Principals* (2003).

Acknowledgments

I would like to thank Chris York, technology director for Del Norte Unified School District in Crescent City, California, for his suggestions and feedback on some of the Excel files. I also want to thank Mathew Manweller, ISTE's former acquisitions editor, who was a driving force behind the publication of my first book, *Making Technology Standards Work for You—A Guide for School Administrators*, and has continued to champion the need for print resources written specifically for school administrators. It has been a joy to work with him again, first on *101 Best Web Sites for Principals* and now on this book.

Contents

Introduction

About This Book

The Electronic Briefcase for Administrators: Tools and Templates is a collection of Microsoft Office files designed for site and district school administrators to use as tools to create a starting point for communication, planning, budgeting, and other administrative tasks. The book includes pointers for using Microsoft Office as well as step-by-step directions for using templates developed specifically for use with Microsoft Office programs. The templates are contained on the CD-ROM included with the book.

The analogy of a briefcase is used because users can open the book and find the particular template that's just right for a specific job, just as it's possible to reach into a briefcase and take out an important file folder or document. No matter where a template appears in the book, by reading the directions and accessing the appropriate template file on the CD-ROM, users have all the necessary information to successfully use the template.

Why does a school administrator need *The Electronic Briefcase for Administrators?* Time is a precious commodity for any school administrator, a commodity that is becoming increasingly difficult to protect. Demands placed upon administrators at both site and central offices far exceed the expectations of even 2 or 3 years ago. Therefore, this book incorporates many of the technologies available today to automate tasks and save time, enabling administrators and their staff to work more efficiently.

Increasing numbers of school administrators possess at least basic word processing and Internet skills. Some have a general idea about how to work with a spreadsheet or create a presentation using such software programs as PowerPoint. However, possessing basic skills is one thing. Having the time and experience to develop templates that make maximum use of these programs is another. A resource such as

The Electronic Briefcase, which provides ready-to-use templates geared to common administrative tasks, is worth its weight in gold.

The book's text, with its step-by-step directions, shows how to automate traditional paper and pencil tasks using technology. The templates will help administrators use data manipulation techniques to make better use of available information when reviewing test scores, overseeing budgets, and performing other types of analyses. Anyone who knows how to open and save files, point and click to access commands, and place a cursor for data entry will be able to use the templates found on the CD-ROM. Even highly skilled users of software programs who know how to develop templates will find these files and the extended-use suggestions valuable time-savers.

How do you use *The Electronic Briefcase?* This is not a book designed for reading cover to cover. Instead, it's a resource of timely tools to be used on an ongoing basis. The templates and program tools are all related to tasks school administrators have responsibility for completing. They are organized around the six themes of the National Educational Technology Standards for Administrators (NETS•A): Leadership and Vision; Learning and Teaching; Productivity and Professional Practice; Support, Management, and Operations; Assessment and Evaluation; and Social, Legal and Ethical Issues.

You will find templates for tasks such as planning programs, conducting an observation of a technology-based lesson, publishing student and faculty handbooks, projecting and monitoring budgets, planning evaluations, and preparing an Internet safety plan presentation for the community. Some of the templates may be used in conjunction with one another. For example, chapter 3 has templates for building a meeting agenda, creating a sign-in sheet, designing a PowerPoint presentation based on the agenda, and taking formal meeting minutes.

So, transfer the template files from the CD-ROM to your computer. If you need assistance with this, turn to the section of this introduction titled Getting Started With the Templates, which describes how to copy files to a PC or Macintosh. To review topics available in each chapter, refer to the Contents or the beginning of every chapter. Each chapter opens with a list of the National Educational Technology Standards for Administrators (NETS•A) and performance indicators that form its theme. This is followed by a table that gives the title for each template, the name of the software program used, and the correlating performance standards. A brief explanation of the purpose for each template is provided in the section titled About This Template. Read through the explanations to identify the templates and tools you will put to immediate use and those that will be needed later. The next time you need to complete a task related to them, simply access the file and use the directions in the text to get the job done. The section titled Microsoft Office Pointers for Beginners provides some additional tips for entry-level users of software programs. As you gain experience using the various program tools, you will also be able to adapt and modify the files to suit your personal style.

Please note: Creating these templates is not meant to imply that administrators need to become their own administrative assistants. However, the reality is that often the line between clerical and administrative tasks is blurred. Understaffed offices, increased workloads, and ready access to technology-based tools often result in people pitching in to do jobs they might not have tackled in the past. In addition to using these templates yourself, many times it will be more appropriate for you to discuss what you need and then have office staff or teacher leaders themselves use the template. For example, if you decide to use the Classroom/Department Expenditures Form tool (chapter 4) to track budgets, you might have a clerk do the data entry and then use the file yourself to generate a chart. Or you may find you share a file with one or more staff members as you work together on a specific task, such as program planning or evaluation design. Because you're all using the same file, you can avoid common problems caused by varying formats or inconsistent data entry. The benefit is the flexibility to use the file with the appropriate person at the appropriate time.

In addition to its place in school or central offices, *The Electronic Briefcase for Administrators* is ideal for professional-development workshops and administrative-credentialing courses, or any other setting where educators are learning how to maximize their time through the use of technology-based tools. Because each template is aligned with the NETS•A, this book provides practical exercises for administrators or intern administrators who are following a professional-growth action plan designed to assist them in becoming proficient technology leaders.

About the NETS for Administrators (NETS•A)

The Technology Standards for School Administrators were developed by the Collaborative for Technology Standards for School Administrators (TSSA Collaborative), a group of educators from across the United States, and published in November 2001. At the same time, the International Society for Technology in Education (ISTE) released the National Educational Technology Standards for Administrators (NETS•A). In terms of actual standards and performance indicators, TSSA and NETS•A are identical. ISTE's long-term goal is to expand upon the TSSA document to include other important information for administrators, including resources such as this book, that administrators can use to implement the standards.

The standards are indicators of specific technology-related skills effective school administrators need in the 21st century. They represent a national consensus of the things PK–12 school administrators need to know and do to effectively support technology integration in schools and go beyond personal productivity or a technology plan. The underlying assumption is that administrators who rely on support staff or teachers to handle technology-related tasks for them lose many of the benefits afforded by access to, and use of, technology. Those administrators who master the use of technology themselves increase their potential to become creative, dynamic leaders in a technology-based environment.

The six broad areas addressed in the standards provide a context that encourages administrators to use their leadership skills and expertise to promote instructional programs which support student outcomes, incorporating technology use where appropriate.

National Educational Technology Standards for Administrators

I. Leadership and Vision

Educational leaders inspire a shared vision for comprehensive integration of technology and foster an environment and culture conducive to the realization of that vision. Educational leaders:

A   facilitate the shared development by all stakeholders of a vision for technology use and widely communicate that vision.

B   maintain an inclusive and cohesive process to develop, implement, and monitor a dynamic, long-range, and systemic technology plan to achieve the vision.

C   foster and nurture a culture of responsible risk-taking and advocate policies promoting continuous innovation with technology.

D   use data in making leadership decisions.

E   advocate for research-based effective practices in use of technology.

F   advocate on the state and national levels for policies, programs, and funding opportunities that support implementation of the district technology plan.

II. Learning and Teaching

Educational leaders ensure that curricular design, instructional strategies, and learning environments integrate appropriate technologies to maximize learning and teaching. Educational leaders:

A   identify, use, evaluate, and promote appropriate technologies to enhance and support instruction and standards-based curriculum leading to high levels of student achievement.

B   facilitate and support collaborative technology-enriched learning environments conducive to innovation for improved learning.

C   provide for learner-centered environments that use technology to meet the individual and diverse needs of learners.

D   facilitate the use of technologies to support and enhance instructional methods that develop higher-level thinking, decision-making, and problem-solving skills.

E provide for and ensure that faculty and staff take advantage of quality professional learning opportunities for improved learning and teaching with technology.

III. Productivity and Professional Practice

Educational leaders apply technology to enhance their professional practice and to increase their own productivity and that of others. Educational leaders:

A model the routine, intentional, and effective use of technology.

B employ technology for communication and collaboration among colleagues, staff, parents, students, and the larger community.

C create and participate in learning communities that stimulate, nurture, and support faculty and staff in using technology for improved productivity.

D engage in sustained, job-related professional learning using technology resources.

E maintain awareness of emerging technologies and their potential uses in education.

F use technology to advance organizational improvement.

IV. Support, Management, and Operations

Educational leaders ensure the integration of technology to support productive systems for learning and administration. Educational leaders:

A develop, implement, and monitor policies and guidelines to ensure compatibility of technologies.

B implement and use integrated technology-based management and operations systems.

C allocate financial and human resources to ensure complete and sustained implementation of the technology plan.

D integrate strategic plans, technology plans, and other improvement plans and policies to align efforts and leverage resources.

E implement procedures to drive continuous improvement of technology systems and to support technology replacement cycles.

V. Assessment and Evaluation

Educational leaders use technology to plan and implement comprehensive systems of effective assessment and evaluation. Educational leaders:

A use multiple methods to assess and evaluate appropriate uses of technology resources for learning, communication, and productivity.

B use technology to collect and analyze data, interpret results, and communicate findings to improve instructional practice and student learning.

C assess staff knowledge, skills, and performance in using technology and use results to facilitate quality professional development and to inform personnel decisions.

D use technology to assess, evaluate, and manage administrative and operational systems.

VI. Social, Legal, and Ethical Issues

Educational leaders understand the social, legal, and ethical issues related to technology and model responsible decision-making related to these issues. Educational leaders:

A ensure equity of access to technology resources that enable and empower all learners and educators.

B identify, communicate, model, and enforce social, legal, and ethical practices to promote responsible use of technology.

C promote and enforce privacy, security, and online safety related to the use of technology.

D promote and enforce environmentally safe and healthy practices in the use of technology.

E participate in the development of policies that clearly enforce copyright law and assign ownership of intellectual property developed with district resources.

Getting Started With the Templates

This section provides information about software program requirements, copying the template files onto a hard drive, and opening and saving files. A table shows what the templates and tools are used for and the chapter each is found in.

Program Requirements

The template files are intended for use with the following Microsoft Office programs (versions 2000 or later).

- Word

- Excel

- PowerPoint

These programs must be installed on your computer to make the best use of the template files. While the files may work with other software programs, the explanations provided in the text are specific to Microsoft Office.

 Look for this icon to see which programs and what equipment you need in order to use each template.

The chapters in this book offer step-by-step instructions for managing the templates.

 When Macintosh directions differ, this icon appears.

Additionally, the text is illustrated with helpful screen shots. Screen shots come from both PCs and Macs.

Managing Templates

What is a template? It's a file that has certain elements or information predefined. Using a template is a great time-saver when regularly using a document with a prede-termined format, such as a weekly bulletin, or when saving data over a period of time in a form, such as a student discipline file or an annual budget-tracking sheet. In the strictest sense, even blank documents are a form of template because default style settings are contained within the file. Files that have been saved using a Document Template format are stored by default in a special Templates folder. Because of their format, these files cannot be overwritten under normal circumstances.

If you are familiar with the Templates folder and are comfortable stashing files there and accessing them later, then you already know how to open any of the files provided in this book and save them as Document Templates. However, those readers not at that skill level can simply open any of the files using the directions given below, then use the Save As option under File on the menu bar to change the file name to avoid overwriting the original file.

Not to worry, however. Even if you forget to use Save As and change information in the original file copied to the hard drive, there is a backup copy of each file on the CD-ROM. The only way to damage the files on the CD-ROM is to physically break the disc!

Copying Files to the Hard Drive

The CD-ROM accompanying this book includes all of the template files described in the book. Each file can be found in the folder named for the corresponding chapter where the template is described. Before using the files, copy them onto your computer. Place the CD-ROM in the disk drive and open it by double-clicking on its icon, which appears in the My Computer window on a PC or on the Desktop on a Macintosh.

To copy a folder and all its contents onto the hard drive using a PC:

1 Right-click on the icon of the folder you want to copy.

2 Scroll down to Send To in the window that appears, then click on My Documents in the pop-up window.

3 The folder and files will be copied into the My Documents folder.

To copy a folder and all its contents onto the hard drive using a Macintosh:

1 Click on the icon of the folder you want to copy and drag the icon onto the Desktop.

Once the folders are copied onto the hard drive, keep the CD-ROM in a safe place for use as a backup. This is in case an original file is accidentally overwritten or lost.

Opening Template Files

To open an Office file using a PC, or to open a PowerPoint file on a Macintosh that has this program installed:

1 Double-click on the My Documents folder on the Desktop (Mac users: skip this step).

2 Find the folder you copied from the CD-ROM and double-click on its icon to open it.

3 Locate the icon for the file you wish to open and double-click on it.

4 The Office program for that file launches automatically and opens the file (Mac users: this technique is for PowerPoint files only).

Newer Macintosh computers come with AppleWorks installed. Microsoft Office may need to be purchased separately and installed.

To open a Word or Excel file using a Macintosh that has both Office and AppleWorks installed, do not simply double-click on the file's icon because the computer may try to convert Word and Excel documents into AppleWorks files. Follow these directions:

1   Open the program for the file (i.e., Word or Excel).

2   Place the cursor on File on the menu bar and click one time.

3   Scroll down to Open and click one time.

4   A window appears that allows you to navigate to your folder on the Desktop.

5   Double-click on the icon for the folder you wish to open, and then double-click on the name of the file.

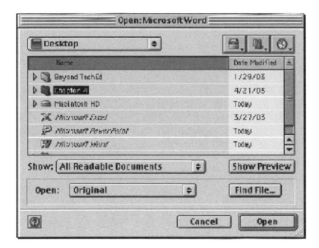

NOTE Hard drives may be configured in a variety of ways, and it's nearly impossible to anticipate every possible place a program might be found. If you do not know how to open a program on your computer, ask someone on your site for assistance.

Saving Template Files

Remember that a file needs to be renamed the first time you save it to avoid overwriting the original on the hard drive. Now that you have copied the folder(s) onto the hard drive and opened a file saved in a folder on the hard drive, your files will be saved there. To rename a file using a PC or a Macintosh:

1   Place the cursor on File on the menu bar and click one time to see the drop-down menu.

2   Scroll down to Save As and click one time.

3   A window appears that shows the contents of the folder where the original file is saved. In the window you see File name: or Save As: with the name highlighted.

4 Type a new name for the modified file that makes sense and that you will remember later.

5 The modified file is now saved in the folder with the original. You may open it later and modify the file again without renaming it, unless for some reason you want multiple copies of your modifications.

NOTE Some template files, such as Meeting Sign-In Sheet, will be modified frequently. This is an instance in which multiple copies of modifications (one for each meeting) would be appropriate.

Viewing Template Files

You may want to make the page on the computer screen appear larger or smaller. To get a closer look at a document or to make more of the document appear on the screen, use the Zoom command. Follow these steps:

1 Place the cursor on View on the menu bar and click one time to see the drop-down menu.

2 Scroll down to Zoom and click one time.

3 A window appears that shows the Zoom defaults (i.e., 200%, 100%, 75%) and a box where you may type a percentage number of your own choosing.

4 Click on a Zoom default size, or type a number in the Percentage box. Click OK.

Using the Templates

The templates are organized by type of task into six chapters that correspond to the National Educational Technology Standards for Administrators (NETS·A).

CHAPTER	TEMPLATES AND TOOLS ARE FOR TASKS RELATED TO:
1 Leadership and Vision	Program planning and evaluation
2 Learning and Teaching	Instruction and professional development
3 Productivity and Professional Practice	General needs, such as a weekly bulletin, certificate, or form letter
4 Support, Management, and Operations	Keeping inventories and budgets
5 Assessment and Evaluation	Needs assessment, data tracking, and reporting
6 Social, Legal, and Ethical Issues	Internet safety, copyright compliance, equal access to programs, and ergonomics issues

Each chapter begins with the text of the NETS•A and its performance indicators. A table shows the performance indicator or indicators supported by each template. Although correlated to the NETS•A and appropriate for use in implementing these standards, the templates themselves are not necessarily limited to technology-specific applications. For example, the template Articulating a Vision, found in chapter 1, can be used to define a vision for technology use in a school, but it may also be used whenever a program vision statement is required.

Template Descriptions

Each chapter uses a consistent format to describe the templates. Following is an explanation of each section included in a description:

About This Template. Explains the purpose of the template.

 Software. Identifies the Office program required for use.

 Additional Equipment. Lists any additional equipment, such as a printer or projection device, needed to get maximum use of the template.

Template View. Illustrates the template.

Directions. Gives step-by-step directions for using the template, which is appropriate for users at all skill levels.

Extensions

More advanced users may want to expand the use of a template by trying these suggested activities.

Microsoft Office Pointers for Beginners

Word

This program enables you to create letters, reports, tables—almost any kind of document you can think of. When using the templates in this book, you are opening an existing document, or one that was created and formatted at a previous time. The following pointers will enhance your use of the templates and software program tools.

WORD INTERFACE

Title bar   Menu bar   Standard toolbar   Formatting toolbar

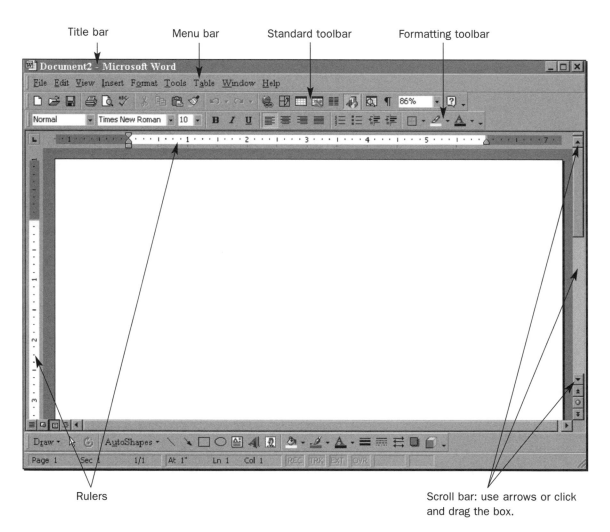

Rulers

Scroll bar: use arrows or click and drag the box.

TITLE BAR

The title bar shows the name of the document you are currently using.

MENU BAR

Click and drag on the various commands listed in the menu bar to see what options are available. Specific instructions are included in the template directions found in each chapter whenever it is necessary to use one of these commands.

STANDARD TOOLBAR

The standard toolbar provides easy access to Word's most frequently used commands.

Because you are working with preexisting documents, you will seldom need to use any of the tools in the standard toolbar. However, the Undo and Redo buttons may come in handy. If you make a mistake, clicking the Undo button (on the left) reverses the last action you took. The Redo button (on the right) is the opposite of Undo.

FORMATTING TOOLBAR

The formatting toolbar contains buttons used to control the appearance of the text in the document and provides access to other formatting operations. Because the documents in this book are preformatted, you will not use these tools unless you are experimenting with some of the suggested activities to expand the use of a template.

TEXT MAGNIFICATION AND REDUCTION

There may be times when you want to either enlarge the text on the screen or see more of an entire document. The Zoom feature allows you to enlarge or reduce the size of the text you are viewing. To access Zoom:

1 Place the cursor on View in the menu bar, click one time, scroll down to Zoom, and click once again.

2 A window appears on the screen. Choose one of the options under Zoom To. Selecting 200% makes the text twice its normal size. Normal size is 100%. Select 75% to make the text smaller so you can see more of the document. There are other choices as well.

3 Click OK.

Excel

This spreadsheet program can be used to calculate budgets, track inventories, and execute other tasks that involve using numbers. Excel can also be used as a database and to generate charts, graphs, and reports. Following are a few pointers for using Excel features when working with the templates and program tools:

EXCEL TERMINOLOGY

Worksheet. An Excel document is called a worksheet. A worksheet consists of up to 256 vertical columns and 65,535 horizontal rows. Columns are identified by letter (A, B, C, etc.) and rows are numbered (1, 2, 3, etc.). Multiple worksheets may be saved in a workbook.

Cell. The intersection of a column and a row is called a cell. Cells are identified by their column and row headings. For example, the first cell is A1.

Label. Labels are used to identify what your numbers mean. Often labels are alpha characters.

Numbers. Numbers are numeric data entered into a cell.

Formulas. Formulas are used to calculate new results based upon the numeric data entered.

EXCEL INTERFACE

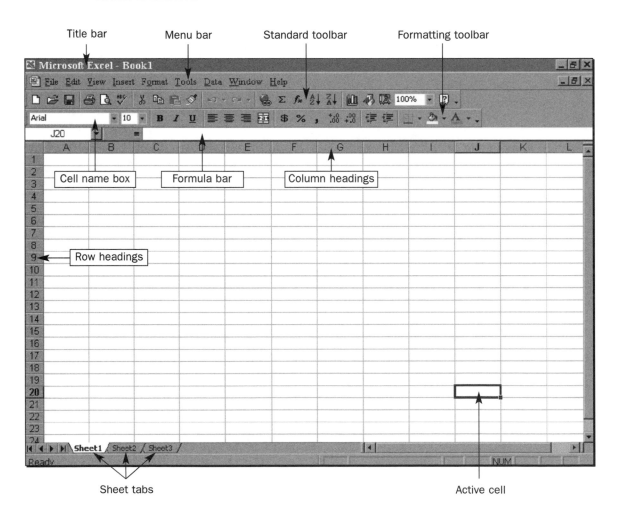

TITLE BAR

The title bar shows the name of the document you are currently using.

MENU BAR

Click and drag on the various commands listed on the menu bar to see what options are available. Specific instructions are included in the template directions in each chapter whenever it is necessary to use one of these commands.

STANDARD TOOLBAR

The standard toolbar provides easy access to Excel's most frequently used commands. Labels indicate tools used when working with the templates and tools found in this book.

Undo and Redo   Ascending/descending sort

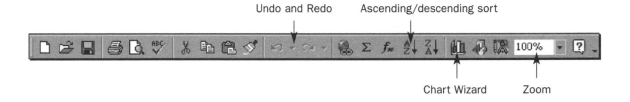

Chart Wizard   Zoom

Because you are working with preexisting worksheets, you will use just a few of the tools in the standard toolbar. Directions provided for the use of each template also include instructions for use of the toolbar.

The Undo and Redo buttons may come in handy. If you make a mistake, clicking the Undo button (on the left) reverses the last action you took. The Redo button (on the right) is the opposite of Undo.

FORMATTING TOOLBAR

This toolbar contains buttons used to control the appearance of the text in the worksheet and provides access to other formatting operations. Because the documents in this book are preformatted, you will not use these tools unless you are experimenting with some of the suggested activities to expand the use of a template.

FORMULA BAR

The formula bar displays what is typed in the active cell. When you enter alpha or numeric data, three symbols appear: a red X, a green checkmark, and an equal sign. Clicking the X deletes the changes you made to the cell. Clicking the checkmark applies the changes to the cell. The cqual sign allows you to edit the content of the cell (typically used when working with formulas).

PowerPoint

PowerPoint is a program used to create visually interesting presentations and handouts. The following pointers will enhance your use of the templates and program tools.

POWERPOINT INTERFACE

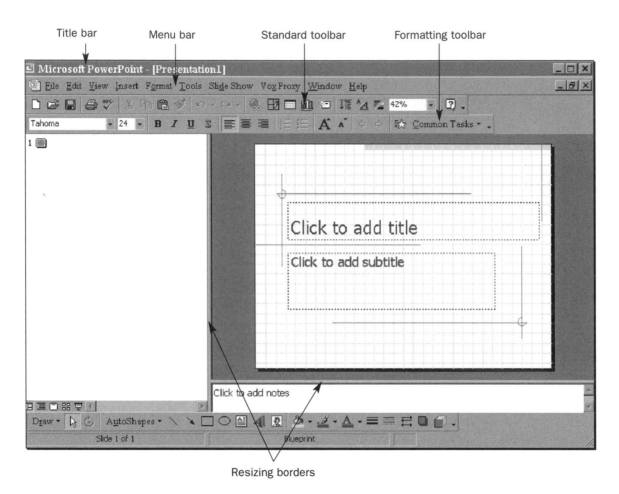

TITLE BAR

The title bar shows the name of the document you are currently using.

MENU BAR

Click and drag on the various commands listed on the menu bar to see what options are available. Specific instructions are included in the template directions found in each chapter whenever it is necessary to use one of these commands.

STANDARD TOOLBAR

The standard toolbar provides easy access to PowerPoint's most frequently used commands.

Because you are working with preexisting presentations, you seldom will need to use any of the tools in the standard toolbar. However, the Undo and Redo buttons may come in handy. If you make a mistake, clicking the Undo button (on the left) reverses the last action you took. The Redo button (on the right) is the opposite of Undo.

FORMATTING TOOLBAR

The formatting toolbar contains buttons used to control the appearance of the text in the presentation and provides access to other formatting operations. Because the documents in this book are preformatted, you will not use these tools unless you are experimenting with some of the suggested activities to expand the use of a template.

VIEWS

The illustration above shows Normal View. Click on View in the menu bar to see additional options for viewing a file.

RESIZING BORDERS

To enlarge or decrease the size of an area you are viewing, place the cursor over one of the resizing borders, then click and drag (right to left, or up and down).

CHAPTER ONE

Leadership and Vision

I. Leadership and Vision

Educational leaders inspire a shared vision for comprehensive integration of technology and foster an environment and culture conducive to the realization of that vision. Educational leaders:

A facilitate the shared development by all stakeholders of a vision for technology use and widely communicate that vision.

B maintain an inclusive and cohesive process to develop, implement, and monitor a dynamic, long-range, and systemic technology plan to achieve the vision.

C foster and nurture a culture of responsible risk-taking and advocate policies promoting continuous innovation with technology.

D use data in making leadership decisions.

E advocate for research-based effective practices in use of technology.

F advocate on the state and national levels for policies, programs, and funding opportunities that support implementation of the district technology plan.

The briefcase contains four word processing templates and one spreadsheet template related to NETS•A I. The chart below lists the templates included in this chapter and indicates the correlation between each template and one or more Standard I performance indicators provided above. In this case, three performance indicators are supported: I.A., I.B., and I.D.

TEMPLATE	PROGRAM	NETS•A I PERFORMANCE INDICATORS					
		I.A.	I.B.	I.C.	I.D.	I.E.	I.F.
Articulating a Vision	Word	●					
Press Release	Word	●					
Program Planner	Word		●				
Evaluation Plan Overview	Word		●		●		
Data Library	Excel				●		

Articulating a Vision

About This Template

School leaders are expected to share with staff members and other stakeholders their vision for instructional programs. However, this requires being able to articulate a personal vision.

This template includes a series of seven questions designed to assist leaders in both identifying their own beliefs and goals for a program and defining strategies for sharing this information with the school's stakeholders. The template may also be used with a Leadership Team to develop a common vision statement.

SOFTWARE	Word
ADDITIONAL EQUIPMENT	printer
	projection device (optional, to be used with a large group)

Template View

Articulating a Vision for Type Name of Program Here

1. My educational vision for my school or district is...	2. My definition of type name of program here is...	3. My definition of type name of program here supports my vision for my school or district in the following ways...

4. The essential elements required to implement my vision:

I have...	I need...

5. Successful strategies I use to share my vision with my staff include...

6. Successful strategies I use to involve my staff in developing a common vision include...
7. Some of the ways I support responsible risk-taking and innovation on the part of my staff include...

Directions

1 Open the template *Articulating a Vision* (Articulating a Vision.doc) found in the Briefcase Chapter 1 folder. (See Getting Started With the Templates in the introduction for directions on opening a template.)

2 Click on View in the menu bar. Scroll down to Header and Footer and click one time. In the header, double-click on the word **Type** in **Type Name of Program Here** to highlight the field, and type the name of the program being considered. For example, Technology Integration, or Mathematics Instruction in Primary Grades. Click on Close in the Header and Footer toolbar.

3 In sections 2 and 3, double-click on the word **type** in **type name of program here** to highlight the text, and type the name of the program in each place. Do not press Enter.

4 To save the file, click once on File in the menu bar, scroll down to Save As, and click one time. Type a name for the file that will make sense later (e.g., My Vision for Technology Integration) and click on the Save button.

5 Enter your answer to each question in the space provided by placing the pointer (cursor) over the blank area and clicking one time. A blinking short vertical line will appear in the space. This line is called an insertion point and shows where letters will appear when you start to type. Type your response to the question. Because this form is a table, the response area will expand automatically if additional space is needed.

6 Save the file from time to time (do not rename the file).

PRINTING THE FORM

7 To print the form, click once on File in the menu bar, scroll down to Print, and click OK.

8 To print a blank form for use offline, complete Steps 1–4 and print the form before answering the questions. You may wish to do this if you want to ask Leadership Team members to answer the questions and do not have computer access for team members.

Extensions

Once you have answered the questions on the template, you might want to

- use either the Highlight or Font Color features on the formatting toolbar to emphasize key words and phrases in your responses to share with a Leadership Team

- ask individual team members to answer the questions and then complete a form jointly, using a projection device and having someone type the group's answers to the seven questions.

Press Release

About This Template

One way to share your vision is to communicate regularly with the community at large by promoting events, activities, and other newsworthy items that underscore that vision. Press releases may be submitted to newspapers, radio stations, and television stations.

This template uses the Forms feature in Word to make it easy to develop press releases. Text is entered in shaded areas called "fields." The remaining text is protected unless you disable a feature called Protect Form. Directions for disabling this protection are provided.

SOFTWARE	Word
ADDITIONAL EQUIPMENT	printer

Template View

Type name of school and/or district here
Type street address here
Type city, state, and zip code here

FOR IMMEDIATE RELEASE

Type name of contact person and telephone number here

Type Headline Here

Type city, state, date here —**Type the lead paragraph, including all main points about the article, here.**

Develop the article more fully in a second paragraph that explains why the item is newsworthy.

Type a concluding statement here, providing contact name and telephone number again.

Directions

1   Open the *Press Release* template (Press Release.doc) found in the Briefcase Chapter 1 folder. (See Getting Started With the Templates in the introduction for directions on opening a template.)

2   Double-click on the first word in the text **Type name of school and/or district here** to highlight the field, then type the information. Press Tab to move to the next field.

3   Pressing Tab highlights the field. You may also double-click on the first word in the text **Type street address** here to highlight the field, then type the information. Press Tab to move to the next field.

4   Pressing Tab highlights the field. You may also double-click on the first word in the text field **Type city, state, and zip code here** to highlight it, then type the information. Press Tab to move to the next field.

5   Pressing Tab highlights the field text. You may also double-click on the first word in the text **Type name of contact person and telephone number here** to highlight the field, then type the information. Press Tab to move to the next field.

6   Pressing Tab highlights the field. You may also double-click on the first word in the text **Type Headline Here** to highlight the field, then type the information. Press Tab to move to the next field.

7   Pressing Tab highlights the field. You may also double-click on the first word in the text **Type city, state, date here** to highlight the field, then type the information. Press Tab to move to the next field.

8   Pressing Tab highlights the field. You may also double-click on the first word in the text **Type the lead paragraph, including all main points about the article, here** to highlight the field, then type the information. The field will expand to accommodate all text entered. Press Tab to move to the next field.

9   Pressing Tab highlights the field. You may also double-click on the first word in the text **Develop the article more fully in a second paragraph that explains why the item is newsworthy** to highlight the field, then type the information. The field will expand to accommodate all text entered. Press Tab to move to the next field.

10 Pressing Tab highlights the field. You may also double-click on the first word in the text **Type a concluding statement here, providing contact name and telephone number again** to highlight the field, then type the information. The field will expand to accommodate all text entered. Press Tab to move to the next field.

DISABLING PROTECTION

11 If you need to change the protected text, disable the form protection by placing the cursor on View in the menu bar, clicking one time, scrolling down to Toolbars, and selecting Forms from the pop-up window.

12 Click one time on the icon that looks like a padlock.

Padlock

13 Make necessary changes by highlighting the protected text you wish to edit and typing the new text.

14 Enable the form protection again by repeating steps 11 and 12 above.

15 To save the file, click once on File in the menu bar, scroll down to Save As, and click one time. Type a name for the file that will make sense later (e.g., Press Release Test Scores 8-10-03) and click on the Save button. The file will be saved in the Briefcase Chapter 1 folder on the hard drive. Remember to save the file frequently while you work (do not rename the file again).

PRINTING THE PRESS RELEASE

16 To print the finished press release, click once on File in the menu bar, scroll down to Print, and click OK. The shading in the fields does not appear when the document is printed.

Extensions

Once you have the hang of using this simple template, you might want to modify the form further to meet press release requirements for local agencies. Remember to disable the form protection before attempting to make changes.

Program Planner

About This Template

Whether you're writing a school site plan, developing a new program, or creating an evaluation and monitoring plan, an excellent mapping tool is a graphic organizer that helps identify the relationship among such elements as goals and outcomes, activities, alignment, assessment tools, professional development needs, and funding sources.

This template is designed for users to analyze individual program goals and their effects on students and teachers as well as to help develop timelines for budget requirements, monitoring, and evaluation. The template includes tables for four goals and four activities for each goal. Directions are provided, however, for adding additional tables or deleting extra activity rows.

The template may be used in conjunction with the *Schoolwide Professional Development Plan* template in chapter 2.

SOFTWARE	Word
ADDITIONAL EQUIPMENT	printer
	projection device (optional, to be used with a large group)

Template View

PROGRAM PLANNER FOR
Type Name of Program Here

Goal: Highlight this text and type the program goal here.

Outcome: Highlight this text and type the outcome here.

Activities	Alignment	Person(s) Responsible	Starting Date	Ending Date
1. Highlight this text and type the activity here.	Highlight this text and type standards here.	Highlight this text and type person(s) responsible here.	Highlight this text and type starting date here.	Highlight this text and type ending date here.
2. Highlight this text and type the activity here.	Highlight this text and type standards here.	Highlight this text and type person(s) responsible here.	Highlight this text and type starting date here.	Highlight this text and type ending date here.
3. Highlight this text and type the activity here.	Highlight this text and type standards here.	Highlight this text and type person(s) responsible here.	Highlight this text and type starting date here.	Highlight this text and type ending date here.
4. Highlight this text and type the activity here.	Highlight this text and type standards here.	Highlight this text and type person(s) responsible here.	Highlight this text and type starting date here.	Highlight this text and type ending date here.

Assessment Tools:	Highlight this text and list assessment tools here.
Professional Development Needs:	Highlight this text and list professional development needs here.
Funding Source(s):	Highlight this text and list funding sources here.

Directions

1 Open the template *Program Planner* (Program Planner.doc) found in the Briefcase Chapter 1 folder. (See Getting Started With the Templates in the introduction for directions on opening a template.)

2 Click on View in the menu bar. Scroll down to Header and Footer and click one time. In the header, double-click on the word **Type** in **Type Name of Program Here** to highlight the field, and type the name of the program (e.g., Language Arts).

3 Still in the header, double-click on the word **Type** in **Type Name of School Here** to highlight the text, and enter the name of the school. Then double-click on the word **Type** in **Type School Year Here** to enter that information. Click on Close in the Header and Footer toolbar.

4 To save the file, click once on File in the menu bar, scroll down to Save As, and click one time. Type a name for the file that will make sense later (e.g., Program Planner for Language Arts) and click on the Save button. The file will be saved in the Briefcase Chapter 1 folder on the hard drive. Remember to save the file frequently while you work (do not rename the file).

5 Click and drag to highlight the field following the word Goal: and enter a program goal.

6 To enter information about outcomes, activities, and so on, highlight the existing text in each table cell as directed and type in your own text. Because these are tables, the columns will automatically resize to fit the text entered.

7 Save the file from time to time (do not rename the file).

INSERTING OR DELETING TABLES

8 If the program includes more than four goals, create a new page for each additional goal. Place the cursor at the bottom of page 1, and click and drag up to the top of the page to highlight both the table and the Goal: field.

9 Place the cursor on Edit in the menu bar, click once, scroll down to Copy and click once again.

10 Now use the scroll bar on the right side of the document to scroll down to the last page in the document. Place the cursor below the existing table on the page and click one time.

11 Place the cursor on Edit in the menu bar, click once, scroll down to Paste and click once again. This creates a new page. If the new Goal: field is at the bottom of a page rather than at the top of the new page, place the cursor above the Goal: field and click one time. Press Enter several times until the field moves down to the next page.

12 If the program includes fewer than four goals, delete extra tables by placing the cursor at the top of the first extra page, then click and drag down to the end of the document. This highlights extra tables and Goal: fields.

13 Place the cursor on Edit in the menu bar, click once, scroll down to Cut and click once again. This deletes the highlighted table(s) and Goal: fields.

14 Save the file (do not rename).

INSERTING OR DELETING ACTIVITY ROWS

The template comes with four activity rows for each outcome. If this is too many, click and drag to highlight the extra rows.

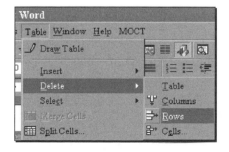

15 Click once on Table in the menu bar, scroll down to Delete, then click on Rows, which appears in the pop-up window. The highlighted rows are now deleted.

16 If additional activity rows are needed, place the cursor over the last row and click one time.

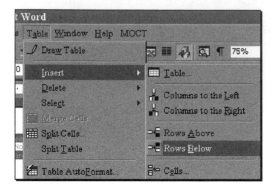

17 Click once on Table in the menu bar, scroll down to Insert and click on Rows Below, which appears in the pop-up window. Repeat to add additional rows.

PRINTING THE FORM

18 To print the *Program Planner*, click once on File in the menu bar, scroll down to Print, and click OK.

Extensions

Once you are familiar with the template, you may want to

- complete the template in small groups, using a projection device and having someone type responses

- modify labels to meet specific program, plan, or district requirements.

Evaluation Plan Overview

About This Template

Once a committee has identified evaluation questions, indicators of success, information sources, criteria or benchmarks for evaluation, and a reporting format, it is helpful to pull the planning and implementation pieces together with a cover document that explains how the plan was developed and the specific information to be collected.

This template uses the Forms feature in Word to allow you to develop an overview for an evaluation and monitoring plan. Text is entered in the shaded fields. The remaining text is protected unless you disable a feature called Protect Form. Directions for disabling this protection are provided.

NOTE This template is most effective if used in conjunction with the *Evaluation Planning Chart* and the *Evaluation Rubric* templates in chapter 5.

| **SOFTWARE** | Word |
| **ADDITIONAL EQUIPMENT** | printer |

Template View

Evaluation Plan Overview
Enter School District Name

Introduction

This overview includes an explanation of how the monitoring and evaluation piece for the enter name of plan here plan was developed. It also includes descriptions of the data to be collected at both the district and site levels as well as a committee roster.

Evaluation Development

An evaluation committee was formed on type the committee formation date here. This group consists of certificated and classified staff of type the name of the school district here, parents, community members, and representatives from local colleges. Committee members and their affiliations are listed in Appendix A.

The committee met several times from type the timespan during which the committee met here to develop evaluation questions, indicators of success, information sources, and criteria and benchmarks. The areas of the type the name of the plan here targeted for this evaluation are: type the components of the plan specifically targeted for evaluation.

Use this field to briefly describe how the committee functioned, e.g., total group, sub-committees, etc.

Evaluation Structure

Implementation of the type the name of the plan here will be monitored and reviewed type the frequency for evaluation, e.g., annually throughout the next type the span of time the plan covers here of the plan's cycle. Data will be collected annually in type the months when data is to be collected here, and reported in type the month when the report will be made here.

The annual report consists of a completed rubric, narrative about how ratings were selected for each area, and supporting documentation. The lead person at the district level is type lead person's name and title here. She is responsible for working with the sites and district personnel to oversee data collection. She will also work with the committee to develop the annual reports. Each site needs to designate a lead person who will collect data and work with type lead person's name here as needed.

The annual report will be presented to the District's Board of Education each type name of month here.

Data Collection
School Sites

The following table describes data to be collected by the school sites and identifies those responsible for collecting and submitting the data.

Item	Description/Person(s) Responsible
Type name of item here.	Describe the item here. Type the title(s) of the person(s) responsible for collecting the item here.
Type name of item here.	Describe the item here. Type the title(s) of the person(s) responsible for collecting the item here.
Type name of item here.	Describe the item here. Type the title(s) of the person(s) responsible for collecting the item here.
Type name of item here.	Describe the item here. Type the title(s) of the person(s) responsible for collecting the item here.
Type name of item here.	Describe the item here.

Appendix A.

Evaluation Committee Members		
Name	Title	Affiliation
Type name here	Type title here	Type affiliation here
Type name here	Type title here	Type affiliation here
Type name here	Type title here	Type affiliation here
Type name here	Type title here	Type affiliation here
Type name here	Type title here	Type affiliation here
Type name here	Type title here	Type affiliation here
Type name here	Type title here	Type affiliation here
Type name here	Type title here	Type affiliation here
Type name here	Type title here	Type affiliation here
Type name here	Type title here	Type affiliation here
Type name here	Type title here	Type affiliation here
Type name here	Type title here	Type affiliation here
Type name here	Type title here	Type affiliation here
Type name here	Type title here	Type affiliation here
Type name here	Type title here	Type affiliation here
Type name here	Type title here	Type affiliation here
Type name here	Type title here	Type affiliation here
Type name here	Type title here	Type affiliation here
Type name here	Type title here	Type affiliation here
Type name here	Type title here	Type affiliation here

Directions

ENTERING INITIAL INFORMATION

1   Open the *Evaluation Plan Overview* template (Evaluation Plan Overview.doc) found in the Briefcase Chapter 1 folder. (See Getting Started With the Templates in the introduction for directions on opening a template.)

2   The Forms feature of Word enables a user to enter specified local information in shaded fields within a prewritten document. To enter your own text in the first field, double-click on the first word in the text **Enter School District Name** to highlight the field, then type the school district name. Press Tab to move to the next field.

3   Pressing Tab highlights the field. You may also double-click on the first word in the text **enter name of plan here** to highlight the field, then type the plan name. Press Tab to move to the next field.

4   Continue entering your own text in each field in the sections titled Evaluation Development and Evaluation Structure. Note that there are two places in the Evaluation Structure section where a drop-down box appears when the field is highlighted. Click on the appropriate selection, then press Tab (see illustration below).

5   To save the file, click once on File in the menu bar, scroll down to Save As, and click one time. Type a name for the file that will make sense later (e.g., Evaluation Plan Overview 2003–06) and click on the Save button. The file will be saved in the Briefcase Chapter 1 folder on the hard drive. Remember to save the file frequently while you work (do not rename the file).

DATA COLLECTION TABLES

6   The next two sections in the file are tables for identifying what data is to be collected at the district and site levels, and by whom. Enter information in the tables using the same technique described above. Double-click on the first word in the text **Type name of item here** to highlight the field, then type the name of the information source (e.g., Student Attendance Records).

7 Press Tab to move to the next field, or double-click on the first word in the text **Describe the item here** to highlight the field, then type a description of the information source (e.g., Attendance records for Grades 4–8 for the 2003–04 school year).

8 Press Tab to move to the next field, or double-click on the first word in the text **Type the title(s) of the person(s) responsible for collecting the item here** to highlight the field, and then type the title(s) of the person(s) responsible for collecting the information, such as the Director of Pupil Personnel Services. Because people may change positions, it is best not to use specific names. Press Tab to move to the next field and continue adding text.

Padlock

9 The tables include space for eight information sources. If more are required, first disable the form protection by placing the cursor on View in the Menu bar, clicking one time, scrolling down to Toolbars, and selecting Forms from the pop-up menu.

10 Click one time on the icon that looks like a padlock.

11 Scroll down to the last row in the table area and click one time.

12 Place the cursor on Table in the menu bar, click one time, scroll down to Insert, and select Rows Below. Click one time. Repeat this step to add the number of additional rows required.

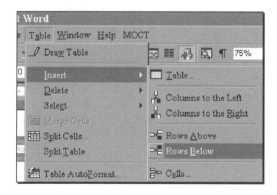

13 Enable the form protection again by repeating steps 9 and 10 above.

14 If fewer than eight rows are needed, first follow steps 9 and 10 to disable the form protection.

15 Click and drag to highlight the extra rows.

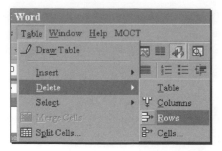

16 Place the cursor on Table in the menu bar, click one time, scroll down to Delete, and select Rows. Click one time to delete the extra rows.

17 Enable the form protection again by clicking one time on the padlock icon in the Forms toolbar (see steps 9 and 10 above).

APPENDICES AND COMMITTEE ROSTER

18 The last two template pages are for listing appendices, such as the committee roster, and the completed templates *Evaluation Planning Chart* and the *Evaluation Rubric* found in chapter 5. Appendix A is the list of committee members (a table is provided to include this information). For Appendix B, double-click on the first word in the text **Type title here** to highlight the field and add a title. Press Tab to move to the field for Appendix C.

19 To add titles for additional appendices, follow steps 9 and 10 to disable the form protection. Type the new titles.

20 Enable the form protection again by repeating steps 9 and 10.

21 The committee roster is another table. Follow steps 6–8 to add information on this table. If you need to add or delete rows, see steps 9–17.

22 Save the file (do not rename the file).

PRINTING THE EVALUATION PLAN OVERVIEW

23 To print the completed file, click once on File in the menu bar, scroll down to Print, and click OK. The shading in the fields does not appear when the document is printed.

Extensions

Once you get   the hang of using this simple template, you might want to modify the form further to better meet local needs. Remember to disable the form protection before attempting to make changes.

Data Library

About This Template

Increased reporting requirements necessitate that administrators have access to a variety of information sources for use in planning, program implementation, and evaluation. In addition to accessing student information, it's important to identify other resources, such as school plans, reports, grant proposals, surveys, inventories, budgets, and so on. It's helpful for administrators to know what artifacts are available to them and where to locate this information quickly. Creating a library of available resources makes the job easier.

Although created in Excel, this template functions as a database. As different data sources are identified, enter information about what the source is, where it can be found, whom to contact, and the date. When you need to track down a specific resource or type of resource quickly, use the Sort or Filter functions to identify items that meet the need and determine where to get them.

SOFTWARE	Excel	
ADDITIONAL EQUIPMENT	printer	

Template View

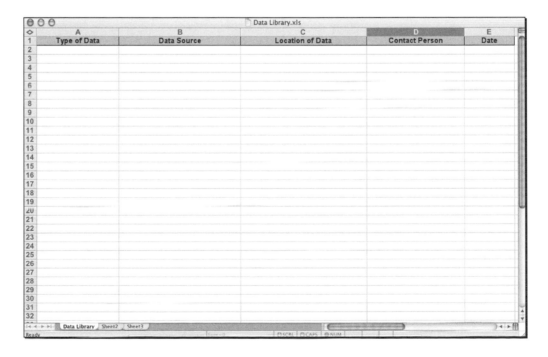

Directions

Open the template *Data Library* (Data Library.xls) found in the Briefcase Chapter 1 folder. (See Getting Started With the Templates in the introduction for directions on opening a template.)

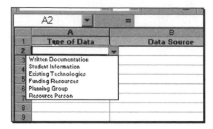

1 To enter data into the worksheet, place the cursor over a cell (A2 for the first entry) and click once. Notice the black arrowhead that appears to the right of the cell.

2 Click once on the arrowhead to see a drop-down list of choices for entries for this cell.

3 Scroll down the list and click on the appropriate choice to enter this information. It's important to enter valid data in this column so that later searches and filters find all the entries related to a particular type of data. Using the drop-down list ensures consistency in data entry.

4 Press the right arrow on the keyboard to move the cursor to cell B2. Type the data source (e.g., School Site Plan, District Writing Test, Current Budget), and press the right arrow to move to the next cell.

5 Continue entering data in this manner in columns C–E. Note that the date format for column E is mm/dd/yy.

6 Repeat in subsequent rows, as needed. See sample below.

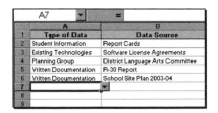

7 To save the file, click once on File in the menu bar, scroll down to Save As, and click one time. Type a name for the file that will make sense later (e.g., Data Library 2003–04) and click on the Save button. The file will be saved in the Briefcase Chapter 1 folder on the hard drive. Remember to save the file frequently while you work, but do not rename the file.

MODIFYING DATA TYPES

8 If you need to add other data types to the drop-down list, place the cursor over the column heading A and click one time. Place the cursor on Data in the menu bar, click once, scroll down to Validation, and click once again.

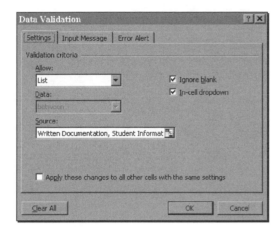

9 Make certain that List is selected under Allow (click on the black arrowhead, scroll down to List, and click one time if it is not currently selected).

10 Place the cursor in front of the W in Written, click once, and type the additional data type(s). Be sure to add a comma after each new data type. Click OK when finished.

11 The new data types will now appear in the drop-down list.

12 Remember to save the modified worksheet but do not rename the file.

MANIPULATING THE DATA

In addition to keeping a list of available data sources, the value of this type of file lies in the basic data manipulation that can be used to generate reports and find listed resources quickly.

Two data manipulation techniques are described below: sorting and filtering.

The sample above shows a worksheet that includes a few entries.

Sorting

13 Notice that the dates are not in chronological order. To view data sources by date, place the cursor over cell E1 (Date) and click one time.

14 Click on the Sort Ascending button in the standard toolbar, or click on Data in the menu bar and select Sort, then click OK in the window that appears. The data are now displayed in chronological order (earliest to latest) as shown below:

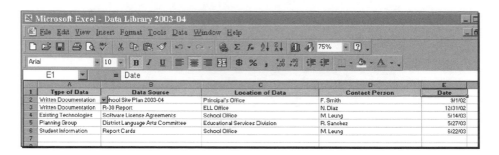

15 A sort of this type may be used in any column heading in row 1.

16 Unless new data were entered during the time the file was open, it is not necessary to save before closing.

Filtering

Filtering makes it possible to view only those entries that meet certain criteria, for example, Written Documentation.

17 To use the AutoFilter feature, click on cell A1 and drag to highlight the row through cell E1.

18 Click on Data in the menu bar and scroll down to Filter. A pop-up menu appears. Select and click on AutoFilter.

19 Drop-down boxes with black arrowheads appear in cells A1 through E1. Cell A1 has two arrowheads because of the Data Validation feature being used. Click on the first arrowhead in cell A1 and read the choices given. The list that appears includes all the different kinds of data in cells in column A. To view only the Written Documentation, scroll down to Written Documentation and click one time.

20 To see all entries again, select (All) from the list.

21 You may filter the list setting criteria in any of the columns.

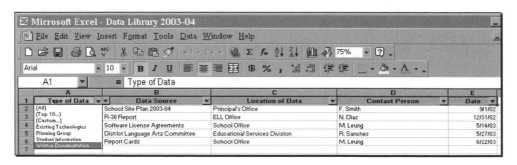

22 To remove the AutoFilter, place the cursor on Data in the menu bar, click and scroll down to Filter. Select and click on AutoFilter in the pop-up menu that appears.

23 Unless new data were entered during the time the file was open, it is not necessary to save before closing.

PRINTING THE WORKSHEET

24 To print the *Data Library*, click once on File in the menu bar, scroll down to Print, and click OK.

Extensions

Once you are familiar with the template, you may want to

- modify the worksheet further by adding additional columns for other information you want to track. Use the Insert command on the menu bar to add columns.

- experiment with combining sorts and filters to generate very specific reports.

CHAPTER TWO

Learning and Teaching

II. Learning and Teaching

Educational leaders ensure that curricular design, instructional strategies, and learning environments integrate appropriate technologies to maximize learning and teaching. Educational leaders:

A identify, use, evaluate, and promote appropriate technologies to enhance and support instruction and standards-based curriculum leading to high levels of student achievement.

B facilitate and support collaborative technology-enriched learning environments conducive to innovation for improved learning.

C provide for learner-centered environments that use technology to meet the individual and diverse needs of learners.

D facilitate the use of technologies to support and enhance instructional methods that develop higher-level thinking, decision-making, and problem-solving skills.

E provide for and ensure that faculty and staff take advantage of quality professional learning opportunities for improved learning and teaching with technology.

The briefcase contains six word processing templates related to NETS•A II. The chart below lists the templates included in this chapter and indicates the correlation between each template and one or more Standard II performance indicators provided above. In this case, all five performance indicators are supported.

TEMPLATE	PROGRAM	II.A.	II.B.	II.C.	II.D.	II.E.
Web Site Evaluation Rubric	Word	●				
Walkthrough Notes	Word		●			
Technology Supported Lesson Observation	Word		●	●	●	
Technology Supported Lesson Plan	Word		●	●	●	
Schoolwide Professional Development Plan	Word					●
Workshop Evaluation	Word					●

NETS•A II PERFORMANCE INDICATORS

Web Site Evaluation Rubric

About This Template

Web sites vary greatly in design and quality. It is helpful for staff members to discuss the elements of design and level of quality they expect to find in Web sites they use with students. Based upon the criteria listed in a discussion of this type, staff members can then develop a mutually acceptable rubric for reviewing Web sites for classroom use.

This template uses the Forms feature in Word to create a rubric once criteria have been established. Text is entered in the shaded areas, called "fields." The remaining text is protected unless you disable a feature called Protect Form. Directions for disabling this protection are provided.

To complete the initial rubric design with a large group, use a computer and projection device so that everyone can see the form and discuss and enter items together.

SOFTWARE	Word
ADDITIONAL EQUIPMENT	printer
	projection device (optional)

Template View

Web Site Evaluation Rubric			
Name of Web Site: Type name of Web site here			
URL: Type Web site address here			
Web Site Design			
Topic	3	2	1	0
Appearance of Page(s)	Enter descriptors here for page(s) that exceed expectations.	Enter descriptors here for page(s) that meet expectations.	Enter descriptors here for page(s) that meet some expectations.	Enter descriptors here for page(s) that do not meet expectations.
Type score here.	Comments: Enter comments here.			
Ease of Navigation	Enter descriptors here for page(s) that exceed expectations.	Enter descriptors here for page(s) that meet expectations.	Enter descriptors here for page(s) that meet some expectations.	Enter descriptors here for page(s) that do not meet expectations.
Type score here.	Comments: Enter comments here.			
Ease of Use	Enter descriptors here for page(s) that exceed expectations.	Enter descriptors here for page(s) that meet expectations.	Enter descriptors here for page(s) that meet some expectations.	Enter descriptors here for page(s) that do not meet expectations.
Type score here.	Comments: Enter comments here.			
Match to Target Audience	Enter descriptors here for page(s) that exceed expectations.	Enter descriptors here for page(s) that meet expectations.	Enter descriptors here for page(s) that meet some expectations.	Enter descriptors here for page(s) that do not meet expectations.
Type score here.	Comments: Enter comments here.			
Web Site Content			
Topic	3	2	1	0
Expertise of Web Site Author	Enter descriptors here for page(s) that exceed expectations.	Enter descriptors here for page(s) that meet expectations.	Enter descriptors here for page(s) that meet some expectations.	Enter descriptors here for page(s) that do not meet expectations.
Type score here.	Comments: Enter comments here.			

Enter criteria for rubric in yellow cells.

Use white cells to enter information when using the completed rubric to evaluate a Web site.

Directions

1 Open the *Web Site Evaluation Rubric* template (Web Site Evaluation Rubric.doc) found in the Briefcase Chapter 2 folder. (See Getting Started With the Templates in the introduction for directions on opening a template.)

2 The blank rubric found on this template includes a rating scale from 0 to 3, with 0 being "do not meet expectations" and 3 being "exceed expectations."

3 Discuss the criteria important in the appearance of a Web page, for example, whether the page is uncluttered and the fonts are easy to read. Use the criteria to create descriptors for a Web page that would exceed, meet, somewhat meet, or not meet the criteria. Enter the four lists of descriptors in the cells for Appearance of Page(s). To begin, double-click on the first word in the text **Enter descriptors here for pages(s) that exceed expectations** to highlight the field, then type these descriptors. Press Tab to move to the next field. Continue until all descriptors for each list are entered.

4 Discuss the criteria important for ease of navigation of a Web site, including moving from one page to the next and being able to return to the Home page easily. Use the criteria to create descriptors for a Web page that would exceed, meet, somewhat meet, or not meet the criteria. Enter the four lists of descriptors in the cells for Ease of Navigation. To begin, double-click on the first word in the text **Enter descriptors here for pages(s) that exceed expectations** to highlight the field, then type these descriptors. Press Tab to move to the next field. Continue until all descriptors for each list are entered.

5 Discuss the criteria important for ease of use of a Web site, for example whether it works with multiple browsers and whether the links work. Use the criteria to create descriptors for a Web page that would exceed, meet, somewhat meet, or not meet the criteria. Enter the four lists of descriptors in the cells for Ease of Use. To begin, double-click on the first word in the text **Enter descriptors here for pages(s) that exceed expectations** to highlight the field, then type these descriptors. Press Tab to move to the next field. Continue until all descriptors for each list are entered.

6 Discuss the criteria important in deciding whether a Web site is appropriate for a particular target audience, for example, its readability and appropriate grade-level content. Use the criteria to create descriptors for a Web page that would exceed, meet, somewhat meet, or not meet the criteria. Enter the four lists of descriptors in the cells for Match to Target Audience. To begin, double-click on the first word in the text **Enter descriptors here for pages(s) that exceed expectations** to highlight the field, then type these descriptors. Press Tab to move to the next field. Continue until all descriptors for each list are entered.

7 Discuss the criteria that would be used to determine the credibility of a Web site author, for example, identification of an author who is known in the field or a

section titled About Us that includes a resumé or other documentation about the author. Use the criteria to create descriptors for a Web page that would exceed, meet, somewhat meet, or not meet the criteria. Enter the four lists of descriptors in the cells for Expertise of Web Site Author. To begin, double-click on the first word in the text **Enter descriptors here for pages(s) that exceed expectations** to highlight the field, then type these descriptors. Press Tab to move to the next field. Continue until all descriptors for each list are entered.

8   Discuss the criteria important in determining the purpose of a Web site, for example, free of bias or intended for instructional use. Use the criteria to create descriptors for a Web page that would exceed, meet, somewhat meet, or not meet the criteria. Enter the four lists of descriptors in the cells for Purpose of Web Site. To begin, double-click on the first word in the text **Enter descriptors here for pages(s) that exceed expectations** to highlight the field, then type these descriptors. Press Tab to move to the next field. Continue until all descriptors for each list are entered.

9   Discuss the criteria important in determining the accuracy of information presented on a Web site, for example, whether the sources cited are well known or whether the site's information can be validated through another source. Use the criteria to create descriptors for a Web page that would exceed, meet, somewhat meet, or not meet the criteria. Enter the four lists of descriptors in the cells for Accuracy of Information Presented. To begin, double-click on the first word in the text **Enter descriptors here for pages(s) that exceed expectations** to highlight the field, then type these descriptors. Press Tab to move to the next field. Continue until all descriptors for each list are entered.

10 Discuss the criteria important in determining the relationship of a Web site to the curriculum being taught, for example whether it is aligned with grade-level content standards and supports the lesson being taught. Use the criteria to create descriptors for a Web page that would exceed, meet, somewhat meet, or not meet the criteria. Enter the four lists of descriptors in the cells for Relationship to Curriculum. To begin, double-click on the first word in the text **Enter descriptors here for pages(s) that exceed expectations** to highlight the field, then type these descriptors. Press Tab to move to the next field. Continue until all descriptors for each list are entered.

11 To save the file, click once on File in the menu bar, scroll down to Save As, and click one time. Type a name for the file that will make sense later (e.g., Web Site Evaluation Rubric 2003–04) and click on the Save button. The file will be saved in the Briefcase Chapter 2 folder on the hard drive.

12 Once the rubric is completed and actually in use, the file should be saved under a different name for each site being evaluated.

MODIFYING THE FORM

13 To change the topics for evaluation, first disable the form protection by placing the cursor on View in the menu bar, clicking one time, scrolling down to Toolbars, and selecting Forms from the pop-up menu.

Padlock

14 Click one time on the icon that looks like a padlock.

15 To change a topic, click and drag to highlight the text to be changed and type the new topic.

16 Enable the form protection again by repeating steps 13 and 14 above.

17 Save the file.

USING THE FORM FOR EVALUATION

18 Once the rubric descriptors are completed, staff may use the form to evaluate Web sites. The fields in white cells are for actual evaluations. Double-click on the word **Type** in the text **Type name of Web site here** to highlight the field. Type the name of the Web site.

19 Double-click on the word **Type** in the text **Type Web site address here** to highlight the field. Type the Web site URL.

20 Read the descriptors for Appearance of Page(s) and choose the score that best matches the site being reviewed. Double-click on the word **Type** in the text **Type score here** to highlight the field. Type a number from 0 to 3.

21 Double-click on the word **Enter** in the text **Enter comments here** to highlight the field. Add any comments about the appearance.

22 Repeat steps 20 and 21 for each evaluation topic.

23 Answer the Yes/No question in the last row by clicking on the appropriate box. If you make a mistake, highlight the box and press the spacebar to remove the X. Double-click on the first word in the text **Enter response here** to highlight the field, and explain your answer.

24 To save the file, click once on File in the menu bar, scroll down to Save As, and click one time. Type a name for the file that will make sense later (e.g., Evaluation of ABC Web Site 12-3-03) and click on the Save button.

PRINTING THE EVALUATION

25 To print the completed rubric, click once on File in the menu bar, scroll down to Print, and click OK. The shading in the fields does not appear when the document is printed.

Extensions

Additional ways to use or modify the template tool might include modifying the form for use in developing a rubric for evaluating software, video, and other instructional materials. Remember to disable the form protection before attempting to make any changes to the form design.

Walkthrough Notes

About This Template

Administrators often choose to maintain high visibility through frequent classroom walkthrough visits. But it's easy to get caught up in unexpected events of a school day and then realize at the end of the week that walkthroughs were either very limited or didn't happen at all.

This template uses the Table feature in Word to allow you to create a form that can be carried on a clipboard and serve as a reminder to drop by a classroom while out on campus. The form also serves as documentation of the walkthroughs done and can be a source of valuable information about classroom instruction trends over time.

SOFTWARE Word

ADDITIONAL EQUIPMENT printer

Template View

Type your name here
Walkthrough Notes for Month of
Type month here

1

Click and type school name here

Room Number	Date/I Saw	Date/I Saw	Date/I Saw
Click and type room number here			
Click and type room number here			
Click and type room number here			
Click and type room number here			
Click and type room number here			
Click and type room number here			
Click and type room number here			

Directions

1 Open the *Walkthrough Notes* template (Walkthrough Notes.doc) found in the Briefcase Chapter 2 folder. (See Getting Started With the Templates in the introduction for directions on opening a template.)

2 Click on View in the menu bar. Scroll down to Header and Footer and click one time. In the header, double-click on the word **Type** in **Type your name here** to highlight the field, and type the name of the person conducting the walkthroughs.

3 Double-click on the word **Type** in **Type month here** to highlight the field, then type the name of the month when the form is used. Click on Close in the Header and Footer toolbar.

4 Triple-click on the text **Click and type school name here** to highlight the field, then type the school's name. Do not press Enter.

5 Triple-click on the text **Click and type room number here** highlight the field, then type the room number. Repeat this step for each classroom.

Look at the sample below:

Susan Brooks-Young Walkthrough Notes for Month of May			1
Anywhere School			
Room Number	**Date/I Saw**	**Date/I Saw**	**Date/I Saw**
K-1			
K-2			
K-3			
K-4			
1			
2			
3			

SAVING THE WALKTHROUGH NOTES

6 To save the file, click once on File in the menu bar, scroll down to Save As, and click one time. Type a name for the file that will make sense later (e.g., Walkthrough Notes May-03) and click on the Save button.

The next month, open the file and change the month in the header. Print the new sheet. You may modify any text by following the directions above.

PRINTING THE WALKTHROUGH NOTES

7 To print your sign-in sheet, click once on File in the menu bar, scroll down to Print, and click OK.

MODIFYING THE WALKTHROUGH NOTES

Deleting Rows

8 The template currently provides space for 40 classrooms and three visits during a month. If there are fewer classrooms, begin the process to delete the extra rows by placing the cursor in the first unneeded row.

9 Click and drag down through all the extra rows to highlight them.

10 Place the cursor on Table in the menu bar, click one time, and scroll down to Delete. Scroll over to Rows in the pop-up window that appears and click one time. The extra rows are then deleted.

Inserting Rows

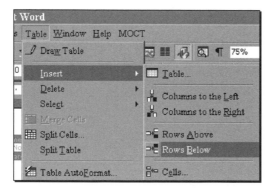

11 If additional rows are required for more than 40 classrooms, place the cursor in the last row in the table on page 2, and click one time. Place the cursor on Table in the menu bar, click one time, and scroll down to Insert. Scroll over to Rows Below in the pop-up window that appears and click one time. An extra row is added. Repeat this step as needed.

Inserting Columns

The template is designed for three walkthroughs per classroom per month. If four are required, add an additional column as follows:

12 Place the cursor over column four and click one time.

13 Click once on Table in the menu bar, scroll down to Insert and click on either Columns to the Left or Columns to the Right in the pop-up window that appears. The table now has four columns for noting observations (five columns total).

14 To copy the formatting for the column heading, triple-click on the text **Date/I Saw** to highlight the field. Click once on Edit in the menu bar, scroll down to Copy and click one time.

15 Place the cursor over the Table cell where you want to add the heading and click one time. Click once on Edit in the menu bar, scroll down to Paste and click one time. Do not press Enter.

16 To center the new heading, place the cursor on Table in the menu bar, click one time, scroll down to Table Properties and click one time.

17 Click on the Cell tab in the window that appears, then click on Center.

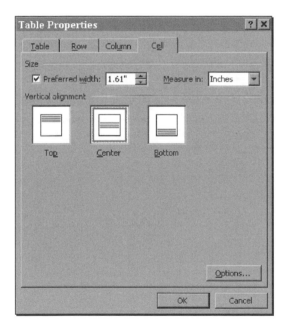

Extensions

Once you have the hang of using this simple template, you might want to

- modify the template when doing walkthroughs to observe a specific instructional strategy or classroom management technique by adding text to the heading to identify exactly what is being observed. This is helpful during program reviews or to document observations when a specific need is identified during an assessment.

- download this template and enter data on your handheld if you have a handheld computer and Documents to Go. This template is then uploaded to your desktop computer the next time the handheld is hot synched.

Technology-Supported Lesson Observation

About This Template

A critical element in helping teachers integrate appropriate use of technology into instruction is to observe classroom activities using a tool that continually directs attention to the question of how technology use supports and enhances content-based activities. This form is designed to help observers and teachers evaluate technology use within the context of academic instruction.

Formal observation forms are nearly always negotiated. Do not use this form for teacher evaluation unless the local bargaining unit has approved it. Instead, use this form in less formal situations where you and the teacher are concentrating on improving technology-based instructional skills. You may, however, keep the important points in mind when formally observing a technology-based lesson.

This template uses the Forms feature in Word and is designed for use on a laptop during an observation. Text is entered in the shaded fields. The remaining text is protected unless you disable a feature called Protect Form. Directions for disabling this protection are provided.

This template may be used in conjunction with the *Technology-Supported Lesson Plan* template, also found in this chapter.

SOFTWARE	Word
ADDITIONAL EQUIPMENT	laptop
	printer

Template View

Technology-Supported Lesson Observation		
Teacher Name: Enter name	**Observer's Name:** Enter name	
Grade Level: Enter grade level	**Start Time:** Enter time	**End Time:** Enter time
Location: e.g., classroom, lab, etc.	**Students Present:** Enter # **Support Staff Present:** Enter #	
Lesson objective(s) clearly defined?	Yes: ☐	No: ☐
Comments: Enter comments here		
Lesson clearly related to Content and Technology Skills Standards?	Yes: ☐	No: ☐
Comments: Enter comments here		
Is technology used to support student learning?	Yes: ☐	No: ☐
Please describe what technology was used and how: Enter comments here, including ways teacher and students used technology		
Describe classroom management techniques used: Explain accommodations made for technology use, student grouping, etc.		
Lesson Introduction		
Lesson introduction was relevant and engaging?	Yes: ☐	No: ☐
Comments: Enter comments here		
Instruction		
Instruction related directly to lesson objective(s)?	Yes: ☐	No: ☐
Instruction was well organized?	Yes: ☐	No: ☐
Technology use *enhanced* instruction?	Yes: ☐	No: ☐
Teacher used opportunities to check for student understanding of concepts?	Yes: ☐	No: ☐
Comments: Enter comments here		
Guided Activity		
Guided activity related directly to instruction and objectives?	Yes: ☐	No: ☐
Technology use *enhanced* guided activity?	Yes: ☐	No: ☐
Teacher monitored students as they worked?	Yes: ☐	No: ☐
Students were able to complete activity with some assistance?	Yes: ☐	No: ☐
Comments: Enter comments here		

Directions

BEFORE THE OBSERVATION

1 Open the *Technology-Supported Lesson Observation* template (Technology-Supported Lesson Observ.doc) found in the Briefcase Chapter 2 folder. (See Getting Started With the Templates in the introduction for directions on opening a template.)

2 Double-click on the first word in the text **Enter name** to highlight the field located in the cell marked Teacher Name, then type the name of the teacher being observed. Press Tab to move to the next field.

3 Pressing Tab highlights the field. You may also double-click on the first word in the text **Enter name** to highlight the field, then type the name of the lesson observer. Press Tab to move to the next field.

4 Pressing Tab highlights the field. You may also double-click on the first word in the text **Enter grade level** to highlight the field, then type the grade level for the class being observed. Press Tab to move to the next field.

5 Pressing Tab highlights the field. You may also double-click on the first word in the text **e.g. classroom, lab, etc.** to highlight the field, then type the location where the lesson is being observed.

6 Read through the remaining information on the form. The form uses a fairly standard lesson-observation format, with the exception of the technology use questions. To modify the form to meet local needs, first disable the form protection by placing the cursor on View in the menu bar, clicking one time, scrolling down to Toolbars, and selecting Forms from the pop-up menu.

7 Click one time on the icon that looks like a padlock.

Padlock

8 To modify headings, click and drag to highlight the text to be changed and type the new text.

9 Enable the form protection again by repeating steps 6 and 7 above.

10 To save the file, click once on File in the menu bar, scroll down to Save As, and click one time. Type a name for the file that will make sense later (e.g., Lesson Observation: Leung—12-4-03) and click on the Save button. The file will be saved in the Briefcase Chapter 2 folder on the hard drive. To transfer the file to a laptop, also save the file on a floppy disk or USB drive. Boot up the laptop and save the file to the hard drive.

DURING THE OBSERVATION

11 Open the file you modified and saved on the laptop hard drive.

12 Double-click on the first word in the text **Enter time** to highlight the field located in the cell marked Start Time, then type the time you begin the observation.

13 Double-click on the first word in the text **Enter #** to highlight the field located in the cell marked Students Present and enter the number of students in the class. Press Tab to move to the next field.

14 Continue working through the form by pressing Tab to highlight a field, then typing the needed information. The default text labels in each field are self-explanatory. Mark the Yes and No boxes by tabbing to the correct box and typing an X. If you mark the wrong box, highlight the box and press the spacebar to remove the X.

15 Remember to save your work from time to time during the observation (but do not rename the file).

PRINTING THE OBSERVATION FORM

16 To print the observation form, click once on File in the menu bar, scroll down to Print, and click OK. The shading in the fields does not appear when the document is printed.

Extensions

If you do not have access to a laptop, you may want to use a hard copy of the form. Open the file and enter the preliminary information as directed above. Tab to the fields that would be filled in during an observation and press the space bar. This temporarily removes the text and causes cells to be blank on the hard copy when printed. You may also want to hit the Enter key one or more times to provide extra space for entering information by hand.

Technology-Supported Lesson Plan

About This Template

Ideally, the use of technology in instruction would be so natural that teachers would not need to focus on how and when to incorporate it. Currently, however, introducing technology into instruction in a meaningful way is a labor-intensive experience for many educators.

Use this form to help teachers consider what they need to think about and do to plan lessons that go beyond both simple automation of lessons taught in the past and teacher-controlled demonstrations using technology. Teachers who are more experienced with technology can use the form to ensure they continue to explore methods for integrating technology seamlessly throughout the day.

The form can also be used as a tool for pre- and post-observation conferences.

This template uses the Forms feature in Word. Text is entered in the shaded fields. The remaining text is protected unless you disable a feature called Protect Form. Directions for disabling this protection are provided.

This template may be used in conjunction with the *Technology-Supported Lesson Observation* template, also found in this chapter.

SOFTWARE   Word

ADDITIONAL EQUIPMENT   printer

Template View

Technology-Supported Lesson Plan
Grade(s) Enter grade level(s)

Time Required: Enter time required to teach complete lesson	**Materials:** List all necessary materials including technology-based items
Content Area Standards and Performance Indicators: Enter each standard and its supporting performance indicator(s)	**Technology Skills Standards and Performance Indicators:** Enter each standard and its supporting performance indicator(s)

Lesson Objective(s): List objective(s)

Technology Is Used to Support Student Learning in the Following Ways:

Describe specifically how technology is incorporated into the lesson and how this supports student learning

How the Teacher Uses Technology: Describe how and when the teacher uses technology in the lesson	**How the Students Use Technology:** Describe how and when students use technology in the lesson

Classroom Management Techniques:

Explain accommodations made for technology use, student grouping, etc.

Preparation Before Class:

List all tasks to be completed prior to lesson

Introduction to the Lesson: Enter text here

Instruction: Enter text here

Guided Activity: Enter text here

Independent Activity: Enter text here

Assessment: Enter text here

Lesson Extensions: Enter text here

Directions

1 Open the *Technology-Supported Lesson Plan* template (Technology-Supported Plan.doc) found in the Briefcase Chapter 2 folder. (See Getting Started With the Templates in the introduction for directions on opening a template.)

2 Double-click on the first word in the text **Enter grade level(s)** to highlight the field, then type the target grade level(s) for the lesson. Press Tab to move to the next field.

3 Pressing Tab highlights the field. You may also double-click on the first word in the text **Enter time required to teach complete lesson** to highlight the field, then type the length of time required to complete the lesson. Press Tab to move to the next field.

4 Pressing Tab highlights the field. You may also double-click on the first word in the text **List all necessary materials including technology-based items** to highlight the field, then type the list. Press Tab to move to the next field.

5 Continue working through the form by pressing Tab to highlight a field, then typing the needed information. The default text labels in each field are self-explanatory.

Padlock

6 The form uses a fairly standard lesson design format. To modify the form to meet local needs, first disable the form protection by placing the cursor on View in the menu bar, clicking one time, scrolling down to Toolbars, and selecting Forms from the pop-up menu.

7 Click one time on the icon that looks like a padlock.

8 To modify headings, click and drag to highlight the text to be changed and type the new text.

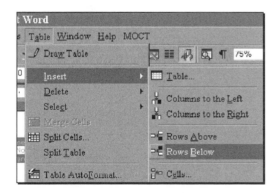

9 To insert rows for additional lesson elements, click in the row above or below the place where a new row should be inserted. Place the cursor on Table in the menu bar. Click one time, scroll down to Insert, and click on Rows Above, or Rows Below in the pop-up window that appears. Repeat until you have inserted the number of rows needed. Type the additional lesson plan elements.

10 If you need to change the number of cells in a row (i.e., go from one cell to two cells), highlight the cell, then use the Merge Cells or Split Cells commands under Table on the menu bar.

11 Enable the form protection again by repeating steps 6 and 7 above.

12 To save the file, click once on File in the menu bar, scroll down to Save As, and click one time. Type a name for the file that will make sense later (e.g., Language Arts Lesson—Verbs) and click on the Save button. The file will be saved in the Briefcase Chapter 2 folder on the hard drive. Remember to save the file frequently while you work (but do not rename it).

PRINTING THE LESSON PLAN FORM

13 To print the lesson plan for distribution, click once on File in the menu bar, scroll down to Print, and click OK. The shading in the fields does not appear when the document is printed.

Extensions

Once you have used this template as a support tool for teachers, you might want to

- consider building a professional library of lesson plans developed in this format that all teachers could access

- encourage teachers to modify the template to meet their individual planning needs.

Schoolwide Professional Development Plan

About This Template

Once a school or program plan is developed, it's helpful to map out the professional development requirements for successfully implementing the plan. Some plans require a separate professional development plan, but even when this is not the case, the plan is a useful tool for tracking dates and funding sources and for use during evaluation.

This template can be used in conjunction with the *Program Planner* template in Chapter 1. Once the *Program Planner* is complete, most of the information required for this template is already available. Identifying the specific professional development activities to support program goals and outcomes would then be the major tasks remaining. The template includes eight rows for goals/outcomes and related professional development; however, directions are provided for inserting or deleting activity rows.

SOFTWARE	Word
ADDITIONAL EQUIPMENT	printer

Template View

Type Name of School Here
Schoolwide Professional Development Plan
Type School Year Here

Goal/ Outcome	Goal/Outcome Implementation Dates	Related Professional Development Activities	Activity Date(s)	Person(s) Attending	Funding Source
Highlight this text type your own.	Highlight this text type dates from plan.	Highlight this text and type the activities here.	Highlight this text and type date(s).	Highlight this text and list attendees here.	Highlight this text and type funding source here.
Highlight this text type your own.	Highlight this text type dates from plan.	Highlight this text and type the activities here.	Highlight this text and type date(s).	Highlight this text and list attendees here.	Highlight this text and type funding source here.
Highlight this text type your own.	Highlight this text type dates from plan.	Highlight this text and type the activities here.	Highlight this text and type date(s).	Highlight this text and list attendees here.	Highlight this text and type funding source here.
Highlight this text type your own.	Highlight this text type dates from plan.	Highlight this text and type the activities here.	Highlight this text and type date(s).	Highlight this text and list attendees here.	Highlight this text and type funding source here.
Highlight this text type your own.	Highlight this text type dates from plan.	Highlight this text and type the activities here.	Highlight this text and type date(s).	Highlight this text and list attendees here.	Highlight this text and type funding source here.
Highlight this text type your own.	Highlight this text type dates from plan.	Highlight this text and type the activities here.	Highlight this text and type date(s).	Highlight this text and list attendees here.	Highlight this text and type funding source here.
Highlight this text type your own.	Highlight this text type dates from plan.	Highlight this text and type the activities here.	Highlight this text and type date(s).	Highlight this text and list attendees here.	Highlight this text and type funding source here.
Highlight this text type your own.	Highlight this text type dates from plan.	Highlight this text and type the activities here.	Highlight this text and type date(s).	Highlight this text and list attendees here.	Highlight this text and type funding source here.

Directions

1 Open the template *Schoolwide Professional Development Plan* (Prof Development Plan.doc) found in the Briefcase Chapter 2 folder. (See Getting Started With the Templates in the introduction for directions on opening a template.)

2 Click on View in the menu bar. Scroll down to Header and Footer and click one time. In the header, double-click on the word **Type** in **Type Name of School Here** to highlight the field and type the school's name.

3 Still in the header, double-click on the word **Type** in **Type School Year Here** to highlight the field, and enter the school year. Click on Close in the Header and Footer toolbar.

4 To save the file, click once on File in the menu bar, scroll down to Save As, and click one time. Type a name for the file that will make sense later (e.g., Schoolwide Professional Development Plan 03-04) and click on the Save button.

5 To enter information about Goal/Outcome, Implementation Dates, Related Professional Development Activities, and so on, highlight the existing text in each table cell, and type in your own text. Because these are tables, the columns will automatically resize to fit the text entered. A convention commonly used for goals and outcomes is to type the goal number, a period, and then the outcome number (e.g., the first outcome for the second goal is 1.1). See the sample below:

		Happy Valley School Schoolwide Professional Development Plan 2003-04				
Goal/ Outcome	Goal/Outcome Implementation Dates	Related Professional Development Activities	Activity Date(s)	Person(s) Attending	Funding Source
2.1	10/1/03–8/15/04	Grade level trainings for new math series adoption in Grades 7–8.	9/1/03	Algebra teachers, Grades 7–8	Title 1

6 Save the file from time to time (do not rename the file).

INSERTING OR DELETING GOAL/OUTCOME ROWS

7 The template comes with eight Goal/Outcome rows. If there are too many rows, click and drag to highlight the extra rows. Click once on Table in the menu bar, scroll down to Delete, then click on Rows, which appears in the pop-up window.

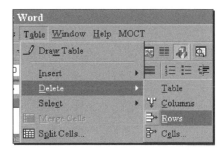

8 If additional Goal/Outcome rows are needed, place the cursor over the last row and click one time. Click once on Table in the menu bar, scroll down to Insert and click on Rows Below, which appears in the pop-up window. Repeat to add additional rows.

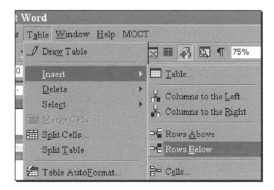

NOTE When the table is complete, it will probably be longer than one page. The template is set to make the table headings appear at the top of each new page.

PRINTING THE FORM

9 To print the *Schoolwide Professional Development Plan*, click once on File in the menu bar, scroll down to Print, and click OK.

Extensions

Once you are familiar with the template, you may want to sort the data in the table by activity date to make notations on the master calendar. Place the cursor in the table and choose Table from the menu bar, then choose Sort and follow the directions to identify the column you want Word to sort by. It's possible to sort by text, number, or date. Try arranging the data by Goal/Outcome, Implementation Dates, or other columns.

Workshop Evaluation

About This Template

Use of a workshop evaluation is common practice, and some evaluations require that professional development paid for by workshop funds be examined and the results included in the evaluation.

Use this template as is to generate a quick evaluation form for any workshops you host, or modify it to meet specific needs.

| SOFTWARE | Word |
| ADDITIONAL EQUIPMENT | printer |

Template View

Type Name of Workshop Here				
Presenter: Type Presenter's Name Here		**Date:** Type Date Here		
We appreciate your attendance at this workshop. Please help us provide quality professional development opportunities for staff by completing this feedback form.				
Current Assignment (please include grade level, if appropriate):				
Site:				
Please mark the appropriate response to each statement below.	Strongly Agree	Agree	Disagree	Strongly Disagree
1. The workshop met my expectations.				
2. The material presented will be helpful in my work.				
3. Adequate time was allowed for the presentation.				
4. The presenter was knowledgeable about the subject matter.				
5. I would recommend this workshop to a colleague.				
Please briefly respond to each of the following statements:				

Directions

1 Open the template *Workshop Evaluation* (Workshop Evaluation.doc) found in the Briefcase Chapter 2 folder. (See Getting Started With the Templates in the introduction for directions on opening a template.)

2 Double-click on the word **Type** in **Type Name of Workshop Here** to highlight the field, and type the name of the workshop.

3 Double-click on the word **Type** in **Type Presenter's Name Here** to highlight the field, and enter the presenter's name.

4 Double-click on the word **Type** in **Type Date Here** to highlight the field, and enter the workshop date.

5 To save the file, click once on File in the menu bar, scroll down to Save As, and click one time. Type a name for the file that will make sense later (e.g., Workshop Evaluation 11-4-03) and click on the Save button.

MODIFYING THE FORM

6 To modify existing text anywhere on the form, highlight the existing text and type in your own. Because this is a table, the rows will automatically resize to fit the text entered. You can also change the descriptors for the 4-point rating scale by clicking on each descriptor and typing new text.

7 The template comes with space for five statements and a 4-point rating scale. If there are too many statements, click and drag to highlight the extra statement rows. Click once on Table in the menu bar, scroll down to Delete, then click on Rows, which appears in the pop-up window.

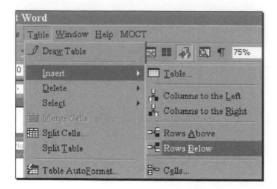

8 To add rows for additional 4-point statements, place the cursor over the last statement row and click one time. Click once on Table in the menu bar, scroll down to Insert and click on Rows Below, which appears in the pop-up window. Repeat to add additional rows.

9 Click in a cell in the first column on the left and type the new statement.

10 The template comes with space for a short response to each of three statements. To delete or add rows for statements of this type, follow the directions provided above.

11 Save the file from time to time (you do not need to rename the file).

PRINTING THE FORM

12 To print the *Workshop Evaluation*, click once on File in the menu bar, scroll down to Print, and click OK.

NOTE The borders in the portion above the 4-point statements are set so that they will not print.

Extensions

Once you are familiar with the template, you may want to experiment with the Merge Cells and Split Cells options under Table on the menu bar to change the rating scale to 3 or 5 points.

3

CHAPTER
THREE

Productivity and Professional Practice

III. Productivity and Professional Practice

Educational leaders apply technology to enhance their professional practice and to increase their own productivity and that of others. Educational leaders:

A model the routine, intentional, and effective use of technology.

B employ technology for communication and collaboration among colleagues, staff, parents, students, and the larger community.

C create and participate in learning communities that stimulate, nurture, and support faculty and staff in using technology for improved productivity.

D engage in sustained, job-related professional learning using technology resources.

E maintain awareness of emerging technologies and their potential uses in education.

F use technology to advance organizational improvement.

The briefcase contains eight word processing templates, one spreadsheet template, and one presentation template related to NETS•A III. The chart below lists the templates included in this chapter and indicates the correlation between each template and one or more Standard III performance indicators provided above. In this case, three performance indicators are supported: III.A., III.B., and III.F.

TEMPLATE	PROGRAM	NETS•A III PERFORMANCE INDICATORS					
		III.A.	III.B.	III.C.	III.D.	III.E.	III.F.
Meeting Agenda Form	Word	●					
Meeting Sign-In Sheet	Word	●					
Meeting Minutes Form	Word	●					
School Letterhead	Word	●					
Daily Bulletin	Word	●	●				
Weekly Bulletin	Word	●	●				
Faculty Handbook	Word	●	●				
Student Handbook	Word	●	●				
Expenses and Mileage Form	Excel	●					●
Staff Meeting Presentation	PowerPoint	●					●

Meeting Agenda Form

About This Template

Meetings with groups such as a School Site Council, parent booster organization, or even a student council require formal agendas.

This template uses the Forms feature in Word to create an agenda quickly. Text is entered in the shaded fields. The remaining text is protected unless you disable a feature called Protect Form. Directions for disabling this protection are provided.

SOFTWARE   Word

ADDITIONAL EQUIPMENT   printer

Template View

> Type Name of School Here
>
> Enter name of committee here
>
> **MEETING AGENDA**
>
> Enter date here
>
>
> **Location:**   Enter meeting location here
> **Time:**   Enter meeting time here
>
> **Call to order**
>
>
> **Approval of Minutes for the Meeting of** Enter date here
>
>
> **Additions to the Agenda**
>
>
> **Information Items:**
>
> List items to be discussed that require no action here

Directions

PREPARING FOR THE MEETING

1 Open the *Meeting Agenda Form* template (Meeting Agenda Form.doc) found in the Briefcase Chapter 3 folder. (See Getting Started With the Templates in the introduction for directions on opening a template.)

2 Double-click on the first word in the text **Type Name of School Here** to highlight the field, then type the school name. Press Tab to move to the next field.

3 Pressing Tab highlights the field. You may also double-click on the first word in the text **Enter name of committee here** to highlight the field, then type the committee name. Press Tab to move to the next field.

4 Pressing Tab highlights the field. You may also double-click on the first word in the text **Enter date here** to highlight the field, then type the meeting date. Press Tab to move to the next field.

5 Pressing Tab highlights the field. You may also double-click on the first word in the text **Enter meeting location here** to highlight the field, then type the meeting date. Press Tab to move to the next field.

6 Pressing Tab highlights the field. You may also double-click on the first word in the text **Enter meeting time here** to highlight the field, then type the meeting time. Press Tab to move to the next field.

7 Use the text entry techniques described above to enter text in the appropriate fields for the date of the minutes being approved; information items; action items; committee reports; and the date, time, and location for the next meeting. The fields will expand to accommodate all text entered.

8 The form includes space for four action items. If more are required, first disable the form protection by placing the cursor on View in the menu bar, clicking one time, scrolling down to Toolbars, and selecting Forms from the pop-up menu.

Padlock

9 Click one time on the icon that looks like a padlock.

10 Scroll down to an action item, and click and drag to highlight the text (see illustration).

```
┌────────────────────────────────┐
│  Action Items:                  │
│                                 │
│                                 │
│   Item: Type item here.         │
│                                 │
│                                 │
│                                 │
│   Item: Type item here.         │
│                                 │
│                                 │
│   Item: Type item here.         │
│                                 │
│                                 │
│                                 │
│   Item: Type item here.         │
│                                 │
└────────────────────────────────┘
```

11 Place the cursor on Edit, click one time, scroll down to Copy, and click once again.

12 Point and click to position the cursor at the point in the document where you want to insert the additional action item.

13 Use the mouse to move the cursor up to Edit on the menu bar, click one time, scroll down to Paste, and click once again. Repeat as needed for extra action items.

14 Enable the form protection again by repeating steps 8 and 9 above.

15 To save the file, click once on File in the menu bar, scroll down to Save As, and click one time. Type a name for the file that will make sense later (e.g., School Site Council Meeting Agenda 5-1-03) and click on the Save button. The file will be saved in the Briefcase Chapter 3 folder on the hard drive. Remember to save the file frequently while you work, but do not rename it.

PRINTING THE MEETING AGENDA FORM

16 To print the agenda, click once on File in the menu bar, scroll down to Print, and click OK. The shading in the fields does not appear when the document is printed.

Extensions

Once you have the hang of using this simple template, you might want to modify the form further. Remember to disable the form protection before attempting to make changes.

Meeting Sign-In Sheet

About This Template

Administrators are often required to document meeting attendance for program evaluations or events sponsored by categorical funds or grants.

This template uses the Table feature in Word to quickly create customized sign-in sheets for any occasion.

SOFTWARE	Word
ADDITIONAL EQUIPMENT	printer

Template View

MEETING SIGN-IN SHEET

Click and type meeting title here

Click and type meeting location here

8/12/03

Click and type column heading here	Click and type column heading here

Directions

1 Open the *Meeting Sign-In Sheet* template (Meeting Sign-In Sheet.doc) found in the Briefcase Chapter 3 folder. (See Getting Started With the Templates in the introduction for directions on opening a template.)

2 Triple-click on the text **Click and type meeting title here** to highlight the field, then type the title of the meeting. Do not press Enter.

3 Triple-click on the text **Click and type meeting location here** to highlight the field, then type the meeting location. Do not press Enter.

4 The current date is automatically entered. If you need to change it, triple-click on the date to highlight the field, then type the correct date.

5 Triple-click on the text **Click and type column heading here** to highlight the field, then type the column heading. Repeat for the second column.

Look at the sample below for a District Parent Advisory Committee meeting:

District Parent Advisory Committee	
Board Room: XYZ School District	
8/6/03	
Parent Name	**School Represented**

SAVING THE SIGN-IN SHEET

6 To save the file, click once on File in the menu bar, scroll down to Save As, and click one time. Type a name for the file that will make sense later (e.g, Parent Sign-In) and click on the Save button.

The next time a sign-in sheet is needed for this group, open the file. The date will automatically change to the current date. If it is the correct date for the meeting and the location is the same, simply print the new sheet. You may modify any text by following the directions above.

PRINTING THE SIGN-IN SHEET

7 To print your sign-in sheet, click once on File in the menu bar, scroll down to Print, and click OK.

MODIFYING THE SIGN-IN SHEET

Deleting Columns

8 Suppose just one column is needed for the sign-in sheet. Place the cursor in one column and click one time.

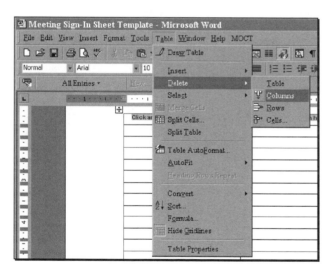

9 Click once on Table in the menu bar, scroll down to Delete and click on Columns in the pop-up window that appears. The table now has just one column.

10 To change the width of the remaining column, place the cursor on one side of the table. When the cursor's appearance changes to a double line with arrowheads on either side, click and drag to increase or decrease the column width.

The sign-in sheet will look like this:

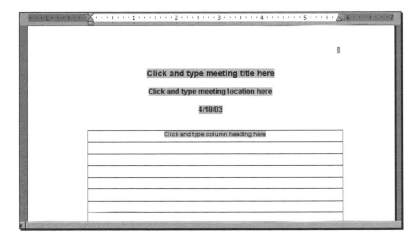

Inserting Columns

11 The sign-in sheet may need additional columns. Place the cursor over one column and click one time.

12 Click once on Table in the menu bar, scroll down to Insert and click on either Columns to the Left or Columns to the Right in the pop-up window that appears. The table now has three columns.

13 To copy the formatting for the column heading, triple-click on the text **Click and type column heading here** to highlight the field. Click once on Edit in the menu bar, scroll down to Copy, and click one time.

14 Place the cursor over the table cell where you want to add the heading and click one time. Click once on Edit in the menu bar, scroll down to Paste, and click one time.

The sign-in sheet will look like this:

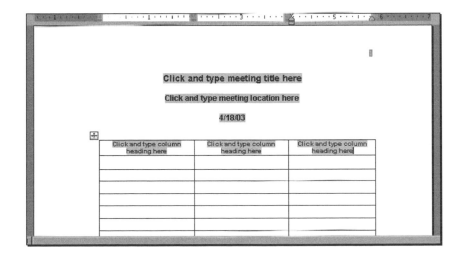

Deleting and Inserting Rows

15 The template comes with 20 rows for signatures. If there are too many rows, click and drag to highlight the extra rows. Click once on Table in the menu bar, scroll down to Delete, then click on Rows, which appears in the pop-up window.

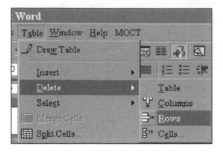

16 If additional rows are needed, place the cursor over the last row and click one time. Click once on Table in the menu bar, scroll down to Insert and click on Rows Below, which appears in the pop-up window. Repeat to add additional rows.

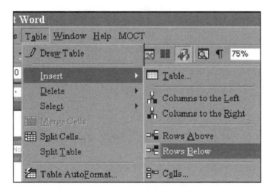

Extensions

Once you have the hang of using this simple template, you might want to dress up the sign-in sheet by adding your school or district logo (assuming you have it saved as a Picture file) or a graphic. Commands for doing this are found under Insert on the menu bar.

Meeting Minutes Form

About This Template

Meetings with groups such as a School Site Council, parent booster organization, or even a student council require that minutes be recorded.

This template uses the Forms feature in Word to help you take formal meeting minutes with ease. Text is entered in the shaded fields. The remaining text is protected unless you disable a feature called Protect Form. Directions for disabling this protection are provided.

SOFTWARE	Word
ADDITIONAL EQUIPMENT	printer

Template View

Type Name of School Here
Enter name of committee here
MEETING MINUTES
Enter date here

Location: Enter meeting location here
Time: Enter meeting time here

The meeting was called to order at Enter starting time here

Members Present: List names here

Members Absent: List names here

Approval of Minutes:

A motion to Enter motion here was made by Enter name here and seconded by Enter name here.

Discussion: Enter discussion points here.

The motion: Passed

The vote was: yes: 0   no: 0   abstaining: 0

Additions to the Agenda:

The motion: Passed

The vote was: **yes:** 0   **no:** 0   **abstaining:** 0

Item: Type item here.
A motion to Enter motion here was made by Type name here
and seconded by Type name here.

Discussion: Enter discussion points here

The motion: Passed

The vote was: **yes:** 0   **no:** 0   **abstaining:** 0

Committee Reports:

List committee name(s), person(s) reporting, and topics mentioned here

Good of the Order:

Enter additional comments here.

Next meeting: Enter date at Enter time and location.

Directions

BEFORE THE MEETING

1 Open the *Meeting Minutes Form* template (Meeting Minutes Form.doc) found in the Briefcase Chapter 3 folder. (See Getting Started With the Templates in the introduction for directions on opening a template.)

2 Double-click on the first word in the text **Type Name of School Here** to highlight the field, then type the school name. Press Tab to move to the next field.

3 Pressing Tab highlights the field. You may also double-click on the first word in the text **Enter name of committee here** to highlight the field, then type the committee name. Press Tab to move to the next field.

4 Pressing Tab highlights the field. You may also double-click on the first word in the text **Enter date here** to highlight the field, then type the meeting date. Press Tab to move to the next field.

5 Pressing Tab highlights the field. You may also double-click on the first word in the text **Enter meeting location here** to highlight the field, then type the meeting location. Press Tab to move to the next field.

6 Pressing Tab highlights the field. You may also double-click on the first word in the text **Enter meeting time here** to highlight the field, then type the meeting time. Press Tab to move to the next field.

7 Before the meeting, use the Meeting Agenda Form to list information items, action items, and anticipated committee reports. Use the text entry techniques described above to enter text in the appropriate fields. The fields will expand to accommodate all text entered.

8 The form includes space for four action items. If more are required, first disable the form protection by placing the cursor on View in the menu bar, clicking one time, scrolling down to Toolbars, and selecting Forms from the pop-up menu.

Padlock

9 Click one time on the icon that looks like a padlock.

10 Scroll down to an action items area, and click and drag to highlight the text (see below).

11 Place the cursor on Edit, click one time, scroll down to Copy, and click once again.

12 Point and click to position the cursor at the point in the document where you want to insert the additional action item information.

13 Use the mouse to move the cursor up to Edit on the menu bar, click one time, scroll down to Paste, and click once again. Repeat as needed for extra action items.

14 Enable the form protection again by repeating steps 8 and 9.

15 To save the file, click once on File in the menu bar, scroll down to Save As, and click one time. Type a name for the file that will make sense later (e.g., School Site Council Minutes 5-1-03) and click on the Save button. The file will be saved in the Briefcase Chapter 3 folder on the hard drive. Remember to save the file frequently while you work, but do not rename it.

DURING THE MEETING

16 Open the file you prepared prior to the meeting. Scroll down to **Enter starting time here.** Double-click on the first word in this field to highlight the field, then type the actual time the meeting was called to order. Press Tab to move to the next field.

17 Pressing Tab highlights the field. You may also double-click on the first word in the text **List names here** to highlight the field, then type the names of members in attendance. Press Tab to move to the next field.

18 Pressing Tab highlights the field. You may also double-click on the first word in the text **List names here** to highlight the field, then type the names of members who are absent. Press Tab to move to the next field.

19 The first action item is the approval of the previous meeting's minutes. See the completed sample below:

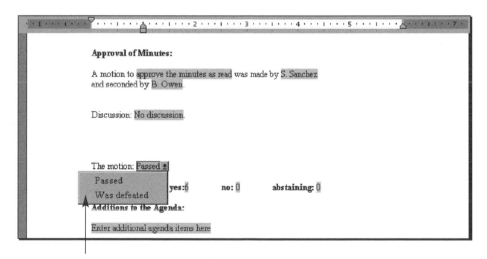

Note drop-down selection for results of vote on a motion.
Scroll to select response.

20 Continue using Tab to move to the next field and enter text. If there are no additional items added to the agenda or there is no discussion on a particular item, type "No items added," or "No discussion," and Tab to the next field.

21 Save the file from time to time, but do not rename it.

PRINTING THE MINUTES FORM

22 To print the completed minutes, click once on File in the menu bar, scroll down to Print, and click OK. The shading in the fields does not appear when the document is printed.

Extensions

Once you have the hang of using this simple template, you might want to

- modify the form further. Remember to disable the form protection before attempting to make changes.

- experiment with the options on the Forms toolbar to create additional drop-down boxes (e.g., to select the name of a person making or seconding a motion rather than typing it each time). Remember to disable the form protection before attempting to make changes.

School Letterhead

About This Template

School administrators often write letters that do not need to be on district letterhead yet require a more formal appearance than do casual notes. Letters of recommendation for staff members or requests for donations from business partners are examples. Some schools may have special letterhead, but often this is not the case.

Use this simple template to generate a school letterhead quickly.

SOFTWARE	Word
ADDITIONAL EQUIPMENT	printer

Template View

Current date automatically inserted here.   School's address goes here.

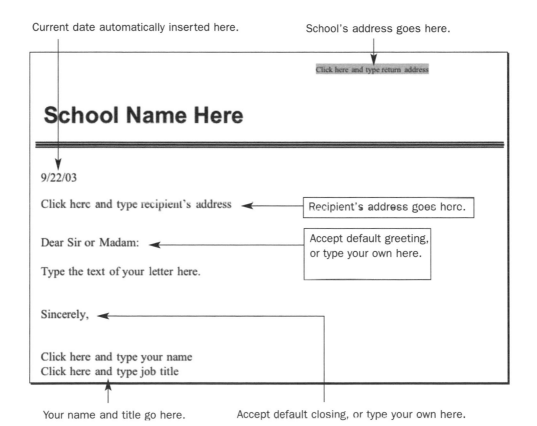

Directions

ADDING THE SCHOOL'S INFORMATION TO THE TEMPLATE

1 Open the *School Letterhead* template (School Letterhead.doc) found in the Briefcase Chapter 3 folder. (See Getting Started With the Templates in the introduction for directions on opening a template.)

2 Triple-click on the text **School Name Here** to highlight the field, then type the school's name. Do not press Enter.

3 Double-click on the first word in **Click here and type return address** to highlight the field, then type the school's return address. Do not press Enter.

4 Click on View in the menu bar. Scroll down to Header and Footer and click one time. Scroll down to the bottom of the page to see the footer. Double-click on the first word in **Click here and type school motto** to highlight the field, then type the school motto. If the school does not have a motto, highlight the text and press Backspace to erase it. Click on Close in the Header and Footer toolbar.

5 Save these basic modifications to the file so that you do not need to reenter the school's information every time you open the file. Place the cursor on File in the menu bar, click one time, scroll down to Save and click one time. (This is one of the rare instances when you want to permanently alter the original file copied from the CD-ROM.)

USING THE TEMPLATE TO WRITE LETTERS

6 Open the *School Letterhead* template found in the Briefcase Chapter 3 folder. (See Getting Started With the Templates in the introduction for directions on opening a template.)

7 The current date is automatically entered. If you need to change it, triple-click on the date to highlight the field, then type the correct date.

8 Triple-click on the text **Click here and type recipient's address** to highlight the field, then type the recipient's address.

9 A generic salutation has been entered. If you wish to change it, triple-click on the text **Dear Sir or Madam** to highlight the field, then type a new salutation.

10 Triple-click on the text **Type the text of your letter here** to highlight the field, then type the letter.

11 A generic closing has been entered. If you wish to change it, triple-click on the text **Sincerely** to highlight the field, then type a new closing.

13 Triple-click on the text **Click here and type your name** to highlight the field, then type your name.

14 Triple-click on the text **Click here and type job title** to highlight the field, then type your job title.

SAVING THE LETTER

15 To save the file, click once on File in the menu bar, scroll down to Save As, and click one time. Type a name for the file that will make sense later (e.g., Smith recommendation) and click on the Save button.

16 The next time you need to write a similar letter, open the file. The date will automatically change to the current date. Make necessary changes in the recipient's address, the body of the letter, etc., then print the new letter and use Save As to change the name of the file and save the new letter without erasing the older file.

PRINTING THE LETTER

19 To print the letter, click once on File in the menu bar, scroll down to Print, and click OK.

Extensions

Once you have the hang of using this simple template , you might want to

- dress up the letterhead by adding your school or district logo (assuming you have it saved as a Picture file) or a graphic. Commands for doing this are found under Insert on the menu bar.

- change the font type, style, or size of the school's name. Highlight the text of the school's name and use the commands under Format and Font in the menu bar.

- change the style of the horizontal line running beneath the school's name. Click on the line to select it. Click on View in the menu bar, scroll to Toolbars, and select Drawing. Click on the Line Style button and select a different line style.

Daily Bulletin

About This Template

Daily bulletins are a communication staple in secondary schools. Whether distributed in print form or electronically as e-mail attachments, daily bulletins serve to keep students and staff members up to date on events and deadlines. They also serve as documentation of events, meeting announcements, and so on. Supervisory duty is assigned in middle schools. High schools may or may not have teachers assigned to daily supervision. Directions for deleting this area are included below.

This template uses the Forms feature in Word to help you create a bulletin easily. Text is entered in the shaded fields. The remaining text is protected unless you disable a feature called Protect Form. Directions for disabling this protection are provided.

See the *Weekly Bulletin* template for elementary school and departmental bulletins.

SOFTWARE	Word
ADDITIONAL EQUIPMENT	printer

Template View

DAILYBULLETIN

	Name of School		
	Date		
Duty Schedule:	Before school	Teacher name	Teacher name
	Nutrition break	Teacher name	Teacher name
	After school	Teacher name	Teacher name
	Bus Duty	Teacher name	Teacher name
From the Principal:	Type activity list here		
From the Assistant Principal(s):	Type activity list here		
From the Counselor(s):	Type activity list here		
From the Student Activities Director:	Type activity list here		
From the Student Council:	Type activity list here		
Departmental Announcements	Type activity list here		
Student Clubs:	Type activity list here		
Sports:	Type activity list here		
	Faculty/Staff Information		
List information just for faculty/staff here			

Directions

1 Open the *Daily Bulletin* template (Daily Bulletin.doc) found in the Briefcase Chapter 3 folder. (See Getting Started With the Templates in the introduction for directions on opening a template.)

2 Double-click on the first word in the text **Name of School** to highlight the field, then type the school name. Press Tab to move to the next field.

3 Pressing Tab highlights the field. You may also double-click on the text **Date** to highlight the field, then type the date. Press Tab to move to the next field.

4 Pressing Tab highlights the field. You may also double-click on the first word in the text **Teacher name** to highlight the field, then type the name of a teacher who has supervisory duty before school. More than one name may be entered in each cell if more than two teachers are assigned supervision at a given time.

5 The next seven fields are also for entering names of teachers who have supervisory duty during the week. Press Tab to move to each field and enter teacher names. If there are additional duty assignments or if the duty assignments are worded differently, see directions provided below for modifying the form.

6 Press Tab or double-click on the first word in the text **Type activity list here** to highlight the field, then type announcements to students from the principal's office. The row will expand as text is added. Press Tab to move to the next field and continue entering announcements from various offices or programs. If nothing is listed for a particular office or program, either type "No activities" or highlight the field and press the spacebar to remove the current text. The shaded area will not appear if the form is printed.

7 Press Tab or double-click on the first word in the text **List information just for faculty/staff here** to highlight the field, then list any faculty/staff announcements or reminders. The row will expand as text is added.

8 To save the file, click once on File in the menu bar, scroll down to Save As, and click one time. Type a name for the file that will make sense later (e.g., Daily Bulletin 11-1-03) and click on the Save button. The file will be saved in the Briefcase Chapter 3 folder on the hard drive. Remember to save the file frequently while you work, but do not rename it.

MODIFYING THE FORM

9 To change the wording for duty assignments, or to add or delete rows for duty assignments, first disable the form protection by placing the cursor on View in the menu bar, clicking one time, scrolling down to Toolbars, and selecting Forms from the pop-up menu.

Padlock

10 Click one time on the icon that looks like a padlock.

11 To change the wording for a duty assignment, click and drag to highlight the text to be changed and type the new text.

12 The template comes with space for four duty assignments, with two teachers for each assignment. If this is too many, click and drag to highlight the extra rows. Click once on Table in the menu bar, scroll down to Delete, then click on Rows, which appears in the pop-up window.

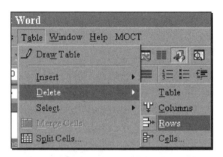

13 To add rows for additional duty assignments, place the cursor over the duty assignment row just above where you want to insert the new row and click one time. Click once on Table in the menu bar, scroll down to Insert and click on Rows Below, which appears in the pop-up window. Repeat to add additional rows.

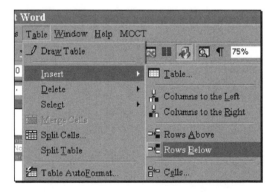

14 Click in a new cell in the column where duties are listed and type the additional title.

15 Click and drag across one of the **Teacher name** fields to highlight it. Place the cursor on Edit in the menu bar, click once and scroll down to Copy. Click once again.

16 Place the cursor over a new cell in one of the columns where teachers' names are entered. Click one time, place the cursor on Edit in the menu bar, click and scroll down to Paste. Click once again. By copying this field into each new cell where a teacher's name is entered, you can access these cells once the form protection is enabled again.

17 Enable the form protection again by repeating steps 9 and 10 above.

18 Save the file.

PRINTING THE DAILY BULLETIN

19 To print the *Daily Bulletin*, click once on File in the menu bar, scroll down to Print, and click OK. The shading in the fields does not appear when the document is printed. The borders for this table are also set so that they will not print.

Extensions

Additional ways to use or modify the template tool might include

- distributing the form electronically rather than in print form. Send it to staff members as an e-mail attachment.

- modifying the form further by adding your school logo. Remember to disable the form protection before attempting to make any changes to the form design.

- adding a quote for the day in the footer on the page. Disable the form protection, and use the Header and Footer option under View in the menu bar.

Weekly Bulletin

About This Template

Weekly bulletins are a primary form of communication between administrators and staff members. Whether distributed in print form or electronically as e-mail attachments, bulletins provide information to staff members and announce events, upcoming meetings, and so on.

This template uses the Forms feature in Word to help you create a bulletin. Text is entered in the shaded fields. The remaining text is protected unless you disable a feature called Protect Form. Directions for disabling this protection are provided.

This template is probably most appropriate for elementary school or departmental use (delete duty schedule rows if used for departments). See the *Daily Bulletin* template, also in this chapter, for middle and high schools.

SOFTWARE	Word
ADDITIONAL EQUIPMENT	printer

Template View

WEEKLY BULLETIN

Name of School		
Week of: Date		

Duty Schedule:	Before School	Teacher name	Teacher name
	First Recess	Teacher name	Teacher name
	Second Recess	Teacher name	Teacher name
	After School	Teacher name	Teacher name
	Bus Duty	Teacher name	Teacher name

Monday:	Type activity list here
Tuesday:	Type activity list here
Wednesday:	Type activity list here
Thursday:	Type activity list here
Friday:	Type activity list here

General Announcements
List general information here

Directions

1 Open the *Weekly Bulletin* template (Weekly Bulletin.doc) found in the Briefcase Chapter 3 folder. (See Getting Started With the Templates in the introduction for directions on opening a template.)

2 Double-click on the first word in the text **Name of School** to highlight the field, then type the school name. Press Tab to move to the next field.

3 Pressing Tab highlights the field. You may also double-click on the first word in the text **Date** to highlight the field, then type the starting date for the week. Press Tab to move to the next field.

4 Pressing Tab highlights the field. You may also double-click on the text **Teacher name** to highlight the field, then type the name of a teacher who has supervisory duty before school. The next nine fields are also for entering names of teachers who have supervisory duty during the week. Press Tab to move to each field and enter teacher names. If there are additional duty assignments, or if the duty assignments are worded differently, see directions provided below for modifying the form.

5 Press Tab or double-click on the first word in the text **Type activity list here** to highlight the field, then type activities, meetings, and so on, scheduled for Monday. The row will expand as text is added. Press Tab to move to the next field, and continue entering information for each day of the week. If nothing is listed for a particular day, either type "No activities" or highlight the field and press the space bar to remove the current text. The shaded area will not appear if the form is printed.

6 Press Tab or double-click on the first word in the text **List general information here** to highlight the field, then list any general announcements. The row will expand as text is added.

7 To save the file, click once on File in the menu bar, scroll down to Save As, and click one time. Type a name for the file that will make sense later (e.g., Weekly Bulletin 9 1 03) and click on the Save button. The file will be saved in the Briefcase Chapter 3 folder on the hard drive. Remember to save the file frequently while you work, but do not rename it.

MODIFYING THE FORM

8 To change the wording for duty assignments, or to add or delete rows for duty assignments, first disable the form protection by placing the cursor on View in the menu bar, clicking one time, scrolling down to Toolbars, and selecting Forms from the pop-up menu.

9 Click one time on the icon that looks like a padlock.

10 To change the wording for a duty assignment, click and drag to highlight the text to be changed, and type the new text.

11 The template comes with space for five duty assignments and two teachers for each assignment. If this is too many, click and drag to highlight the extra rows. Click once on Table in the menu bar, scroll down to Delete, then click on Rows, which appears in the pop-up window.

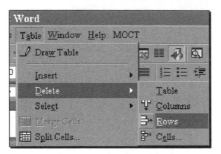

12 To add rows for additional duty assignments, place the cursor over the duty assignment row just above where you want to insert the new row and click one time. Click once on Table in the menu bar, scroll down to Insert and click on Rows Below, which appears in the pop-up window. Repeat to add additional rows.

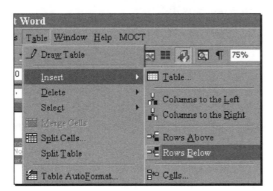

13 Click in a new cell in the column where duties are listed and type the additional title.

14 Click and drag across one of the **Teacher name** fields to highlight the field. Place the cursor on Edit in the menu bar, click once, and scroll down to Copy. Click once again.

15 Place the cursor over a new cell in one of the columns where teacher names are entered. Click one time, place the cursor on Edit in the menu bar, click, and scroll down to Paste. Click once again. By copying this field into each new cell where a teacher's name is entered, you can access these cells once the form protection is enabled again.

16 Enable the form protection again by repeating steps 8 and 9 above.

17 Save the file.

PRINTING THE WEEKLY BULLETIN

18 To print the *Weekly Bulletin*, click once on File in the menu bar, scroll down to Print, and click OK. The shading in the fields does not appear when the document is printed. The borders for this table are also set so that they will not print.

Extensions

Additional ways to use or modify the template might include

- distributing the form electronically rather than in print form. Send it to staff members as an e-mail attachment.

- modifying the form further by adding your school logo. Remember to disable the form protection before attempting to make any changes to the form design.

- adding a quote for the week in the footer on the page. Disable the form protection, and use the Header and Footer option under View in the menu bar.

Faculty Handbook

About This Template

A handbook is an important tool for providing information for faculty members, and it requires updating at least annually.

Use this template to cut down on the time it takes to revise the faculty handbook each year. You may also decide to use this electronic format to post the handbook on your school's Web site for faculty reference. The template uses the Bookmark and Hyperlink capabilities of Word to enable you to move directly from the table of contents to each individual section of the handbook. Directions are provided for removing each section's table borders prior to printing.

SOFTWARE	Word
ADDITIONAL EQUIPMENT	printer

Template View

TITLE PAGE

Faculty Handbook

Name of School
Street Address
City, State Zip Code

Telephone number
Fax number
Web site URL

Office Hours:
Type office hours here

TABLE OF CONTENTS

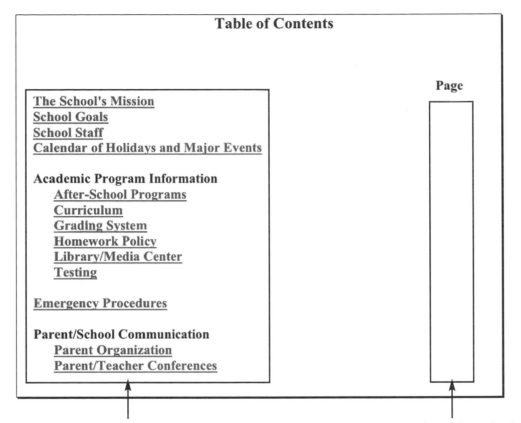

Table of Contents

Page

The School's Mission
School Goals
School Staff
Calendar of Holidays and Major Events

Academic Program Information
  After-School Programs
  Curriculum
  Grading System
  Homework Policy
  Library/Media Center
  Testing

Emergency Procedures

Parent/School Communication
  Parent Organization
  Parent/Teacher Conferences

Click on any link to go directly to that section in the document for text entry or revision.

Type page numbers here after each section is complete and handbook is formatted.

NOTE If you are using the XP version of Word, place the cursor over the link, hold down the Control key and click one time.

Click on the Back arrow to return to the table of contents.

NOTE If you are using the XP version of Word, you must make the Web toolbar visible to see the Back arrow. Place the cursor on View in the menu bar, click one time and scroll down to Toolbars. A pop-up menu will appear. Scroll down to Web and click one time.

HANDBOOK SECTIONS

The School's Mission	
Highlight this text and type your own.	

School Goals	
Highlight this text and type your own.	

School Staff	
Name	Position

Directions

1 Open the template *Faculty Handbook* (Faculty Handbook.doc) found in the Briefcase Chapter 3 folder. (See Getting Started With the Templates in the introduction for directions on opening a template.)

2 Double-click on the first word in **Name of School** to highlight the field, then type the name of the school.

3 Double-click on the first word in **Street Address** to highlight the text, then type the street address for the school.

4 Use this same technique to enter information for the remaining fields on the title page. If your school does not have a Web site, highlight the field and press Backspace to erase the field.

5 To save the file, click once on File in the menu bar, scroll down to Save As, and click one time. Type a name for the file that will make sense later (e.g, Faculty Handbook 2003–04) and click on the Save button.

MODIFYING HANDBOOK SECTIONS

The handbook sections in this template are generic and are usually included in a faculty handbook. However, you may want to make some changes.

6 Scroll through the table of contents to see the sections included in this template. Note that there are five blank tables for extra sections. Decide which sections you will use, which you will delete, and what you need to add.

Deleting a Section

7 Place the cursor over a row in a section table you wish to delete, and click one time. Position the cursor over Table in the menu bar, click one time, scroll down to Delete, and highlight Table in the pop-up window. Click one time. Remember to delete the corresponding title in the table of contents. Click and drag to highlight the title. Place the cursor on Edit in the menu bar, click one time, scroll down to Cut, and click once again.

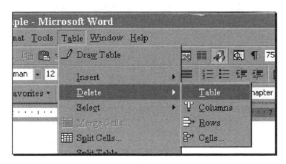

 NOTE Don't forget to delete the blank tables you do not intend to use.

Adding a Section

8 As mentioned above, there are five blank tables for your use. To add a new section, click and drag to highlight the table that needs to be moved, as shown below (use this technique to be certain you pick up the bookmark for that table).

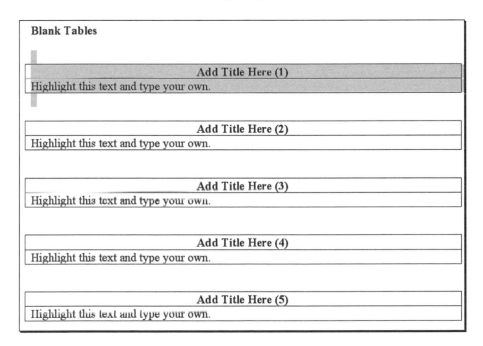

9 Place the cursor on Edit in the menu bar, click one time, scroll down to Cut, and click once again.

10 Scroll up through the document to the place where you want to insert the blank table. Click in the empty space between the existing tables. Place the cursor on Edit in the menu bar, click one time, scroll down to Paste, and click once again. You may need to press Enter or Backspace to adjust spacing.

11 To change the title in a blank table, click and drag to highlight the text **Add Title Here** (1) and type the new title. Notice the number in parentheses. You need to know this number to reestablish the Hyperlink after changing the title in the table of contents.

12 Scroll to the place in the table of contents where you want to insert the title for the blank table you just renamed. Place the cursor just after the title that will be above the title you are inserting. Click one time and press Enter.

13 Type the new title for the blank table, then click and drag to highlight the title. Click on the Hyperlink button on the standard toolbar (see illustration below).

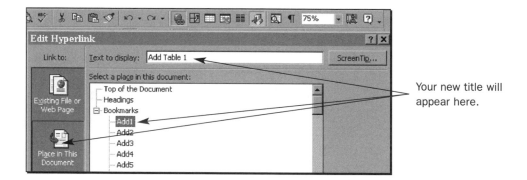

To link the new title to the blank table, click on the Place in This Document button and click on Bookmarks in the box with the heading "Select a place in this document." The bookmarks for the blank tables are called Add1 through Add5, and they will be listed at, or near, the top of the bookmark list. Click on the bookmark with the number that corresponds with the number that was in the title for the blank table. Then click OK.

15 Click on the new title in the table of contents to make sure you picked up the bookmark when you moved the table. If not, use the Undo button in the standard toolbar to move the title and the table back to their original positions and try again. Be careful to highlight the table as shown above before cutting and pasting.

16 Save the file from time to time as you rearrange tables and titles (do not rename the file).

ADDING TEXT

17 Once the handbook section tables are placed, use the Bookmark feature to access each section table and enter text. If you have a previous year's handbook in electronic format, open that file and use Cut and Paste to place the text in the appropriate sections. You may also simply enter the text by highlighting the text **Highlight this text and type your own**, then type the new information.

18 To use the Bookmark feature, scroll through the table of contents to find the title of a specific section and click on that title to move directly to the section. When you finish typing, click on the Back arrow to return to the table of contents and make another selection.

19 To add additional rows to the list of school staff members, place the cursor over the last row in the table and click one time. Position the cursor over Table on the menu bar, click one time, scroll down to Insert, and highlight and click on Rows Below in the pop-up window that appears. Repeat to add as many rows as needed.

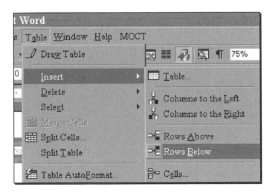

20 Save the file as you work, but do not rename it.

PAGE NUMBERING

21 Once all text is entered, scroll through the document and make adjustments as needed for the placement of text. For example, if you have deleted titles in the table of contents, you may need to use the Backspace or Enter key to align the top of the first section with the top of the page.

22 Page numbers are inserted at the bottom of each page. Use the title links and the Back arrow to check numbering. Place the cursor after each title, press the Tab key, and type the page number for each section.

HIDING TABLE BORDERS

23 To hide borders for a table so that they do not appear in the completed document, click on a table, place the cursor over Table on the menu bar, and click once again. Scroll down to Table Properties and click one time.

Click on **None.**

Select Table.

24 Make sure the Table tab is selected by clicking on it, then click on the button that says Borders and Shading.

25 A window called Borders and Shading appears. Make sure the Borders tab is selected by clicking on it. Click on None under Borders Setting. Select Table in the Apply to: area (click on the arrowhead and scroll down to Table and click one time). Click OK in each window.

PRINTING THE HANDBOOK

26 To print the handbook, click once on File in the menu bar, scroll down to Print, and click OK.

Extensions

Once you have filled out the template, you might want to

- insert a graphic on the title page. Use the Picture command in the Insert command on the menu bar.

- include appendices, such as forms teachers use regularly or copies of such important documents as the Acceptable Use Policy.

Student Handbook

About This Template

A handbook is an important tool for providing information for students and their families, and it requires updating at least annually.

Use this template to cut down on the time it takes to revise the student handbook each year. You may also decide to use this electronic format to post the handbook on your school's Web site for student and parent reference. The template uses the Bookmark and Hyperlink capabilities of Word to enable you to move directly from the table of contents to each individual section of the handbook. Directions are provided for removing each section's table borders prior to printing.

SOFTWARE	Word
ADDITIONAL EQUIPMENT	printer

Template View

TITLE PAGE

Student Handbook

Name of School
Street Address
City, State Zip Code

Telephone number
Fax number
Web site URL

Office Hours:
Type office hours here

TABLE OF CONTENTS

Table of Contents

Page

Welcome Message From the Principal
The School's Mission
School Goals
After-School Programs
Attendance Policy
Bus Transportation
Calendar of Holidays and Major Events
Code of Conduct
Contacting School Staff Members
Curriculum
Daily Schedule
Dress Code
Emergency Cards
Enrolling in School
Field Trips
Grading System
Health Records and Immunization Requirements
Homework Policy

Click on any link to go directly to that section in the document for text entry or revision.

Type page numbers here after each section is complete and handbook is formatted.

 NOTE If you are using the XP version of Word, place the cursor over the link, hold down the Control key and click one time.

Click on the Back arrow to return to the table of contents.

 NOTE If you are using the XP version of Word, you must make the Web toolbar visible to see the Back arrow. Place the cursor on View in the menu bar, click one time and scroll down to Toolbars. A pop-up menu will appear. Scroll down to Web and click one time.

HANDBOOK SECTIONS

Welcome Message from the Principal
Highlight this text and type your own.

The School's Mission
Highlight this text and type your own.

School Goals
Highlight this text and type your own.

After School Programs
Highlight this text and type your own.

Attendance Policy
Highlight this text and type your own.

Bus Transportation
Highlight this text and type your own.

Directions

1 Open the template *Student Handbook* (Student Handbook.doc) found in the Briefcase Chapter 3 folder. (See Getting Started With the Templates in the introduction for directions on opening a template.)

2 Double-click on the first word in **Name of School** to highlight the field, then type the name of the school.

3 Double-click on the first word in **Street Address** to highlight the field, then type the street address for the school.

4 Use this same technique to enter the information for the remaining fields on the title page. If your school does not have a Web site, highlight the field and press Backspace to erase the field.

5 To save the file, click once on File in the menu bar, scroll down to Save As, and click one time. Type a name for the file that will make sense later (e.g., Student Handbook 2003–04) and click on the Save button.

MODIFYING HANDBOOK SECTIONS

The handbook sections in this template are generic and are usually included in a student handbook. However, you may want to make some changes.

6   Scroll through the table of contents to see the sections included in this template. Note that optional sections for both secondary and elementary schools may be added. Decide which sections you will use, which you will delete, and what you need to add.

Deleting a Section

7   Place the cursor over a row in a section table you wish to delete, and click one time. Position the cursor over Table in the menu bar, click one time, scroll down to Delete, and highlight Table in the pop-up window. Click one time. Remember to delete the corresponding title in the table of contents. Click and drag to highlight the title. Place the cursor on Edit in the menu bar, click one time, scroll down to Cut, and click once again.

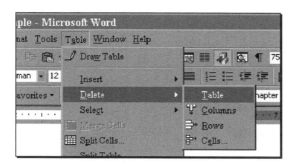

NOTE Don't forget to delete the optional sections and blank tables you do not intend to use.

Adding a Section

8   Several optional sections are available for secondary and elementary schools. Five blank tables are also available for your use. To add an optional section, click and drag to highlight the table that needs to be moved, as shown below (use this technique to be certain you pick up the bookmark for that table).

Blank Tables

Add Title Here (1)
Highlight this text and type your own.

Add Title Here (2)
Highlight this text and type your own.

Add Title Here (3)
Highlight this text and type your own.

Add Title Here (4)
Highlight this text and type your own.

Add Title Here (5)
Highlight this text and type your own.

9 Place the cursor on Edit in the menu bar, click one time, scroll down to Cut, and click once again.

10 Scroll up through the document to the place where you want to insert the blank table for the optional section. Click in the empty space between the existing tables. Place the cursor on Edit in the menu bar, click one time, scroll down to Paste, and click once again. You may need to press Enter or Backspace to adjust spacing.

 NOTE Steps 11 and 12 are for moving titles for the optional section tables. If you have inserted a blank table, please refer to steps 13–17 for directions on entering a title in the table of contents.

11 Scroll up through the document to find the title for the table that was just moved. Click and drag to highlight the title, place the cursor on Edit in the menu bar, click one time, scroll down to Cut, and click once again.

12 Scroll to the place in the table of contents where you want to insert the title. Place the cursor just after the title that will be above the title you are inserting. Click one time and press Enter. Place the cursor on Edit in the menu bar, click one time, scroll down to Paste, and click once again. The title is now inserted. Click on the title to make sure you picked up the bookmark when you moved the table. If not, use the Undo button in the standard toolbar to move the title and the table back to their original positions and try again. Be careful to highlight the table as shown above before cutting and pasting.

MODIFYING A TITLE IN A BLANK TABLE

13 To change the title in a blank table, click and drag to highlight the text **Add Title Here** (1) and type the new title. Notice the number in parentheses. You need to know this number to reestablish the Hyperlink after changing the title in the table of contents.

14 Scroll to the place in the table of contents where you want to insert the title for the blank table you just renamed. Place the cursor just after the title that will be above the title you are inserting. Click one time and press Enter.

15 Type the new title for the blank table, then click and drag to highlight the title. Click on the Hyperlink button on the standard toolbar (see illustration below).

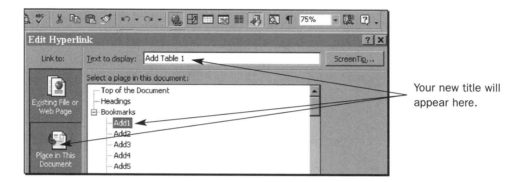

Your new title will appear here.

16 To link the new title to the blank table, click on the Place in This Document button and click on Bookmarks in the box with the heading "Select a place in this document." The bookmarks for the blank tables are called Add1 through Add5, and they will be listed at, or near, the top of the bookmark list. Click on the bookmark with the number that corresponds with the number that was in the title for the blank table. Then click OK.

17 Click on the new title in the table of contents to make sure you picked up the bookmark when you moved the table. If not, use the Undo button in the Standard toolbar to move the title and the table back to their original positions and try again. Be careful to highlight the table as shown above before cutting and pasting.

18 Save the file from time to time as you rearrange tables and titles (do not rename the file).

ADDING TEXT

19 Once the handbook section tables are placed, use the Bookmark feature to access each section table and enter text. If you have a previous year's handbook in electronic format, open that file and use Cut and Paste to place the text in the appropriate sections. You may also simply enter the text by highlighting the text **Highlight this text and type your own**, and then type the new information.

20 To use the Bookmark feature, scroll through the table of contents to find the title of a specific section and click on that title to move directly to the section. When you finish typing, click on the Back arrow to return to the table of contents and make another selection.

21 Save the file as you work, but do not rename it.

PAGE NUMBERING

22 Once all text is entered, scroll through the document and make adjustments as needed for the placement of text. For example, if you have deleted titles in the table of contents, you may need to use the Backspace or Enter key to align the top of the first section with the top of the page.

23 Page numbers are inserted at the bottom of each page. Use the title links and the Back arrow to check numbering. Place the cursor after each title, press the Tab key, and type the page number for each section.

HIDING TABLE BORDERS

24 To hide borders for a table so that they do not appear in the completed document, click on a table, place the cursor over Table on the menu bar, and click once again. Scroll down to Table Properties and click one time.

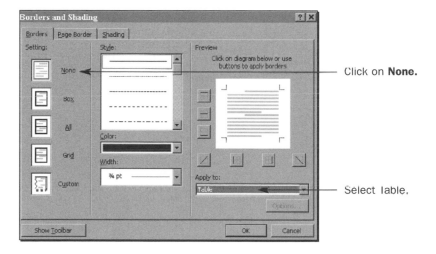

25 Make sure the Table tab is selected by clicking on it, then click on the button that says Borders and Shading.

26 A window called Borders and Shading appears. Make sure the Borders tab is selected by clicking on it. Click on None under Borders Setting. Select Table in the Apply to: area (click on the arrowhead and scroll down to Table and click one time). Click OK in each window.

PRINTING THE HANDBOOK

27 To print the handbook, click once on File in the menu bar, scroll down to Print, and click OK.

Extensions

Once you have filled out the template, you might want to

- insert a graphic on the title page. Use the Picture command in the Insert command on the menu bar.

- include appendices, such as a copy of the Acceptable Use Policy.

Expenses and Mileage Forms

About This Template

Staying on top of out-of-pocket expenses can be trying at times, but expenses do add up quickly, making the time spent keeping records worthwhile.

Use this template to track your out-of-pocket expenditures, both expenses that may be reimbursed through the business office and those that are tax deductions if they are not reimbursed. Separate worksheets are provided for expenses and mileage.

Directions are provided for using a simple filter technique for tracking expenses that are reimbursed and those that are not. Directions are also included for conducting simple sorts and generating subtotals for reports.

SOFTWARE	Excel
ADDITIONAL EQUIPMENT	printer

Template View

EXPENSES WORKSHEET

Data entered in these cells are automatically added to the mileage worksheet as well.

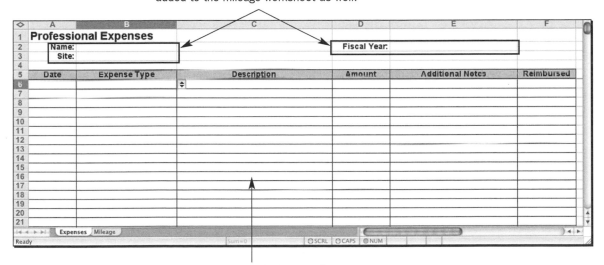

Data are entered in these cells. Use drop-down menus for columns B and F.

MILEAGE WORKSHEET

Data for these cells are automatically added when the same information is entered on the expenses worksheet.

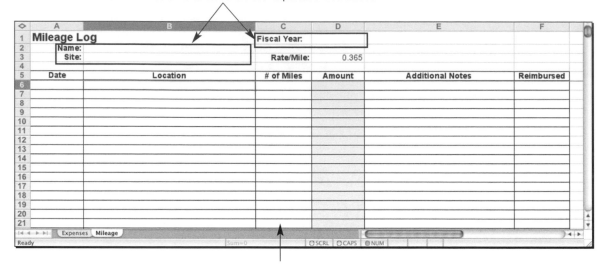

Data are entered into cells in columns A–C and E–F. The amount for column D is automatically calculated.

Directions

INITIAL SETUP

1   Open the template *Expenses and Mileage Forms* (Expenses and Mileage.xls) found in the Briefcase Chapter 3 folder. (See Getting Started With the Templates in the introduction for directions on opening a template.)

2   Click on the Expenses tab in the lower left corner of the Excel window. Place the cursor over cell B2 and click one time. Type your name and press the down arrow or Enter to move the cursor to cell B3. Type the name of the site, and press Enter.

3   Place the cursor over cell E2 and enter the fiscal year being tracked. The information in these three cells is automatically entered into the corresponding cells on the mileage log.

4   Save the file by clicking once on File in the menu bar, scrolling down to Save As, and clicking one time. Type a name for the file that will make sense later (e.g., Expenses 2003–04) and click on the Save button. The file will be saved in the Briefcase Chapter 3 folder on the hard drive. Remember to save the file frequently as you work, but do not rename it.

INSERTING OR DELETING ROWS

Because of the design of this particular template, it is highly unlikely rows will need to be added or deleted. It is possible to enter information for 400 individual items on each sheet.

MODIFYING EXPENSE TYPES

5 If you need to add other expense types to the drop-down list, place the cursor over cell B6 and click one time. Place the cursor on Data in the menu bar, click once, scroll down to Validation, and click once again.

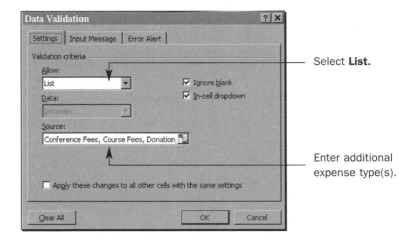

Select **List.**

Enter additional expense type(s).

6 Make certain List is selected under Allow (click on the black arrowhead, scroll down to List, and click one time if it is not currently selected).

7 Place the cursor in front of the C in Conference, click one time, and enter the additional expense type(s). Be sure to add a comma after each new type of expense. Click OK when finished.

8 To make new expense types appear in the drop-down list in cells B7 through B404, Click on B6 and place the cursor over the lower right corner. When the cursor shape changes to a crosshair, click and drag to highlight cells B7–B404.

9 Remember to save the modified worksheet, but do not rename it.

ONGOING USE OF THE SPREADSHEET

Each time you have an out-of-pocket expense or use your personal vehicle for business travel, record the transaction or mileage on the spreadsheet.

10 Open the file you set up and saved and select the appropriate worksheet by clicking on its tab.

Expenses Tab

11 Click on the Expenses tab in the lower left corner of the Excel window. Position the cursor over the first blank cell in column A, click one time, then type the date of the expense. Press the right arrow on the keyboard to move to the next cell in the next column.

12 Select the expense type from the drop-down list, by clicking on the arrowhead that appears on the right side of the cell and scrolling down to the correct item. Click one time.

13 Press the right arrow on the keyboard to move to the next cell in the next column. Type a brief description of the expense.

14 Press the right arrow on the keyboard to move to the next cell in the next column. Type the amount of the expense. Excel will automatically add the dollar sign and decimal point.

15 Use the same technique to add any additional information about the purchase, then choose Yes or No from the drop-down list in column F to indicate whether the expense is reimbursable.

	A	B	C	D	E	F
1	**Professional Expenses**					
2	**Name:** Ester Marquez			**Fiscal Year:** 2003-04		
3	**Site:** Happy Valley School					
4						
5	**Date**	**Expense Type**	**Description**	**Amount**	**Additional Notes**	**Reimbursed**
6	9/6/03	Office Supplies	All You Need Office Supply	$12.00	Marking pens	Yes
7	10/4/03	Office Supplies	All You Need Office Supply	$45.20	Stationery, business cards	Yes
8	12/8/03	Office Supplies	Better Deal Office Supply	$6.53	Index cards	Yes
9	11/2/03	Meal	Burger Joint	$5.50	Dinner meeting with Asst. Supt.	No
10	9/15/03	Conference Fees	Early Literacy Conference	$250.00		Yes
11	9/15/03	Meal	Lunch at Early Literacy Conference	$8.50		No
12	9/5/03	Professional Dues	United School Administrators	$120.00		Yes
13						
14						

Expenses / Mileage

Mileage Tab

16 Click on the Mileage tab in the lower left corner of the Excel window. Check the mileage rate in cell D3. If the rate is correct, proceed to step 17. If the rate is incorrect, click on cell D3 and type the correct rate.

17 Position the cursor over the first blank cell in column A, click one time, then type the date of the travel. Press the right arrow on the keyboard to move to the next cell in the next column.

18 Enter the travel destination, press the right arrow key on the keyboard, then type the total number of miles traveled. Notice that Excel automatically calculates the mileage reimbursement amount for you.

19 Press the right arrow key two times to place the cursor in the column for additional notes. Add any notes and press the right arrow key once again.

20 Choose Yes or No from the drop-down list in column F to indicate whether the expense is reimbursable.

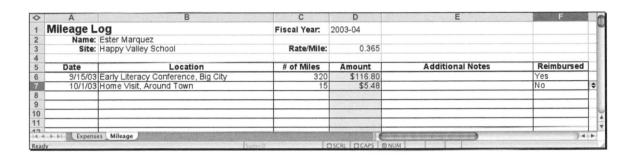

◇	A	B	C	D	E	F
1	Mileage Log		Fiscal Year:	2003-04		
2	Name:	Ester Marquez				
3	Site:	Happy Valley School	Rate/Mile:	0.365		
4						
5	Date	Location	# of Miles	Amount	Additional Notes	Reimbursed
6	9/15/03	Early Literacy Conference, Big City	320	$116.80		Yes
7	10/1/03	Home Visit, Around Town	15	$5.48		No
8						
9						
10						
11						
12						

Expenses | Mileage

Ready

21 Save the file after making the updates.

22 To print a worksheet, click on its tab to make it appear on the screen. Place the cursor on File in the menu bar, click one time, scroll down to Print, then click once again. Click OK in the window that appears.

MANIPULATING THE DATA

In addition to keeping a list of your expenditures and travel, the value of this type of file lies in the ability to manipulate data to generate reports.

Three data manipulation techniques using the sample expenses worksheet are described here: sorting, filtering, and subtotals.

NOTE These techniques may also be used with the mileage worksheet, but first disable the Protection feature for this worksheet by placing the cursor on Tools in the menu bar, clicking one time, and scrolling down to Protection. A pop-up window appears. Scroll over to Unprotect Sheet and click one time.

When you are finished, enable the Protection feature again by accessing Protection under Tools on the menu bar. The option, Protect Sheet, now appears in the pop-up window. Select this option for each worksheet. Do not enter a password when prompted. Click OK.

Sorting

23 Notice that the dates on the expenses sample are not in chronological order. To view data sources by date, place the cursor on cell A5 (Date) and click one time.

24 Click on the Sort Ascending button in the standard toolbar, or click on Data in the menu bar, and select Sort. Click OK in the window that appears. The data are now displayed in chronological order (earliest to latest) as shown below:

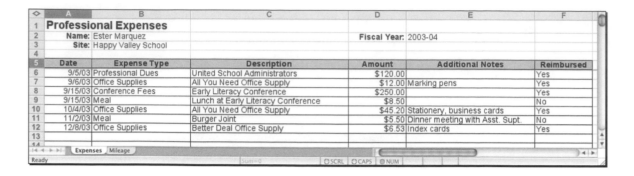

25 A sort of this type may be used in any column heading in row 5 on either worksheet.

26 Unless new data were entered during the time the file was open, it is not necessary to save before closing.

Filtering

Filtering makes it possible to view only those entries that meet certain criteria, for example, office supplies.

27 To use the AutoFilter feature, click on cell A5 and drag to highlight the row through cell F5.

28 Click on Data in the menu bar and scroll down to Filter. A pop-up menu appears. Select and click on AutoFilter.

29 Drop-down boxes with black arrowheads appear in cells A5 through F5. Click on the arrowhead in cell B5 and read the choices given. The list that appears includes all the different kinds of data that are currently used in cells in column B. To view only the office supply expenditures, scroll down to Office Supplies and click one time.

30 To see all entries again, select (All) from the list.

31 You may filter the list setting criteria in any of the columns.

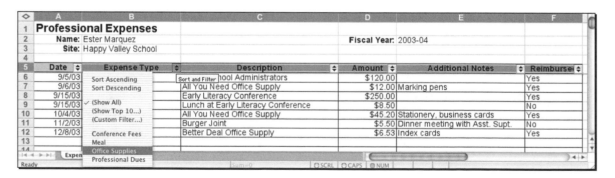

32 To remove the AutoFilter, place the cursor on Data in the menu bar, click and scroll down to Filter. Select and click on AutoFilter in the pop-up menu that appears.

33 Unless new data were entered during the time the file was open, it is not necessary to save before closing.

Subtotals

Subtotals are used with sorted data when values are being tracked. In this expenses and mileage spreadsheet it is useful to subtotal expenditures by expense type or date. This feature offers several subtotal options, including Sum, Average, and Count.

34 To generate subtotals by expense type, first sort the expense type in ascending order (see steps 23 and 24).

35 With cell B5 still selected, place the cursor on Data in the menu bar, click one time, scroll down and click one time to select Subtotals. A window appears (see below). Make sure Expense Type is showing in the box headed "At each change in." Make sure Sum is showing in the box headed "Use function" and that Amount is selected in the box headed "Add subtotal to." If a check mark appears anywhere else in the box headed "Add subtotal to," click on the check mark to remove it, then click OK.

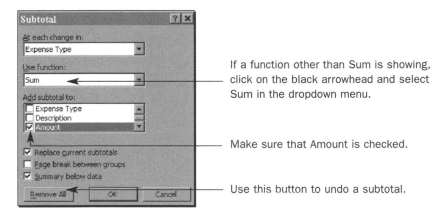

If a function other than Sum is showing, click on the black arrowhead and select Sum in the dropdown menu.

Make sure that Amount is checked.

Use this button to undo a subtotal.

The worksheet now displays entries in alphabetical order by expense type, and a subtotal is inserted each time the expense type changes.

36 To print this worksheet view, move the cursor to File, click one time, scroll down to Print and click OK.

37 To remove the subtotals, click one time on Data, scroll to Subtotals, and click one time. Look for the button in the lower left-hand corner that says Remove All and click on it (see illustration above).

38 Unless new data were entered during the time the file was open, it is not necessary to save before closing.

Extensions

Once you are familiar with the template, you may want to experiment with combining sorts and filters to generate very specific expense reports.

Staff Meeting Presentation

About This Template

Becoming sidetracked is a common occurrence in staff meetings, even if an agenda is being used. Showing visuals can help people stick to the topic and move through the agenda more efficiently.

Use this template during a meeting to highlight important announcements, identify critical points related to each agenda item, and record action items and minutes. Action items and minutes can then be exported into Microsoft Word and printed for distribution to the staff.

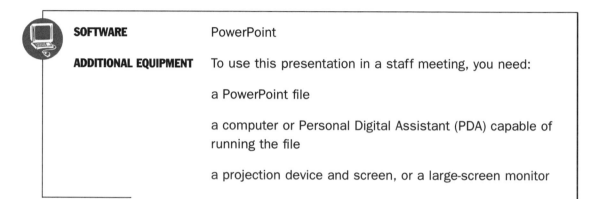

SOFTWARE	PowerPoint
ADDITIONAL EQUIPMENT	To use this presentation in a staff meeting, you need:
	a PowerPoint file
	a computer or Personal Digital Assistant (PDA) capable of running the file
	a projection device and screen, or a large-screen monitor

Template View

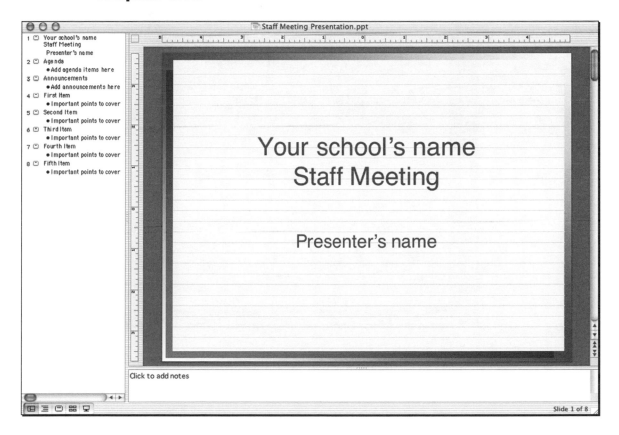

Directions

1 Open the *Staff Meeting Presentation* template (Staff Meeting Presentation.ppt) found in the Briefcase Chapter 3 folder. (See Getting Started With the Templates in the introduction for directions on opening a template.)

2 Click and drag across the text **Your school's name** to highlight the text, then type the name of your school. Do not press Enter.

3 Move the cursor down to click and drag across the text **Presenter's name**. With this text highlighted, type the name of the person chairing the meeting. Do not press Enter.

4 To proceed to slide 2, either click on the scroll-down arrow on the right side of the window or click on slide 2 in the outline pane shown on the left-hand side of the screen.

5 Click and drag across the text **Add agenda items here** to highlight the text, then type the first item and press Enter. The cursor drops down one line, and another check mark appears. Continue adding items.

If there are more than five items, add an additional slide. Place the cursor on Insert in the menu bar and click one time. Scroll down to Duplicate Slide and click one time. This creates a copy of the current slide. Click and drag to highlight the text you want to replace with new text and continue adding items.

6 When the agenda is complete, go to the slide titled First Item (see step 4).

7 Highlight the text **First Item** and type the title for the first agenda item. Do not press Enter.

8 Highlight the text **Important points to cover**, type the first point, and press Enter. The cursor drops down one line and another check mark appears. Continue adding points.

If there are more than five points, add an additional slide. Place the cursor on Insert in the menu bar and click one time. Scroll down to Duplicate Slide and click one time. This creates a copy of the current slide. Click and drag to highlight the text you want to replace with new text and continue adding points.

9 Repeat steps 6–8 to add information about items 2 through 5.

10 If the agenda has fewer than five items, delete the extra slides by moving to the slide(s) you want to delete, clicking once on Edit in the menu bar, scrolling down to Delete Slide, and clicking once again.

SAVING THE PRESENTATION

11 To save the file, click once on File in the menu bar, scroll down to Save As, and click one time. Type a name for the file that will make sense later (e.g., March Staff Meeting) and click on the Save button.

VIEWING THE PRESENTATION

12 To view the presentation, click on Slideshow in the menu bar and scroll down to View Show. Click one time. The first slide appears on the screen.

13 Use the right and left arrow keys to move back and forth through the slides.

ACTION ITEMS AND MEETING MINUTES

14 To record action items or take minutes during the slideshow, right click one time while a slide is displayed. A pop-up menu appears. Click one time on Meeting Minder.

NOTE Macintosh users record action items or take minutes during the slideshow by holding down the Control key and clicking one time while a slide is displayed. A pop-up menu appears. Click one time on Meeting Minder.

15 The Meeting Minder window appears. When the Meeting Minutes tab is selected (as shown below), notes may be typed and later exported into a Word document. When the Action Items tab is selected, notes may be entered concerning who is responsible for certain tasks and deadlines. Action items may also be exported into a Word document. To export minutes or action items, exit the slideshow by pressing the Escape key, click on File, and scroll down to Send to. Click on Microsoft Word in the pop-up window that appears, select from the window the format you want to use, and click OK.

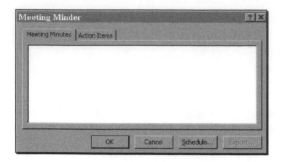

16 When the Action Items feature is used, PowerPoint automatically generates a final slide called Action Items. This slide may be used as a wrap-up for the meeting.

Extensions

Once you have the hang of using this simple template, you might want to

- change slide formats by selecting New Slide instead of Duplicate Slide. You will have 12 slide formats to choose from.

- add pictures or graphs to make a point. Commands for doing this are found under Insert on the menu bar.

- experiment with the various print options available:

    - the Slides option prints one slide per page

    - the Handouts option creates miniature versions of the slides on pages that participants can keep for later reference

    - the Notes Pages option prints the notes for each slide

    - the Outline option prints only the outline format for the presentation.

CHAPTER FOUR

Support, Management, and Operations

IV. Support, Management, and Operations

Educational leaders ensure the integration of technology to support productive systems for learning and administration. Educational leaders:

A develop, implement, and monitor policies and guidelines to ensure compatibility of technologies.

B implement and use integrated technology-based management and operations systems.

C allocate financial and human resources to ensure complete and sustained implementation of the technology plan.

D integrate strategic plans, technology plans, and other improvement plans and policies to align efforts and leverage resources.

E implement procedures to drive continuous improvement of technology systems and to support technology replacement cycles.

The briefcase contains five spreadsheet templates related to NETS•A IV. The chart below lists the templates included in this chapter and indicates the correlation between each template and one or more Standard IV performance indicators provided above. In this case, four performance indicators are supported: IV.B., IV.C., IV.D., and IV.E.

TEMPLATE	PROGRAM	NETS•A IV PERFORMANCE INDICATORS				
		IV.A.	IV.B.	IV.C.	IV.D.	IV.E.
Book Inventories and Orders	Excel		●			
Software Inventory	Excel		●			●
Budget Projection	Excel		●		●	
Budget Tracking Sheet	Excel			●		
Classroom/Department Expenditures	Excel			●		

Book Inventories and Orders Form

About This Template

Whether textbooks are stored in classrooms or a book room, or housed in the Library/Media Center or some other centralized location, both inventories and orders for additional texts are required throughout the year. Unless the site has an automated system that tracks individual books through bar coding, orders and inventories are often based on simple counts of the materials on hand.

Although created in Excel, this template functions as a database. Use this template for both inventories and orders. Once data are entered, the information can be sorted and filtered by teacher name, grade level, room number, type of text, and so on. Subtotals for numbers of books ordered or total numbers of books on hand may also be generated.

	SOFTWARE	Excel
	ADDITIONAL EQUIPMENT	printer

Template View

Book Inventories and Orders										
Grade	Teacher	Rm.	Lang. Arts	T. Manual	Student	Math	T. Manual	Student	Science	T. Manual

Directions

1 Open the template *Book Inventories and Orders* (Book Inventories and Orders.xls) found in the Briefcase Chapter 4 folder. (See Getting Started With the Templates in the introduction for directions on opening a template.)

2 Place the cursor over cell A1 and click one time. Notice that the text for cell A1 appears in the data entry bar. If this is an inventory, place the cursor after the last letter in Order and press the Backspace key six times to remove the word Order and the /. If this is an order, use the same technique to remove Inventory/. You may also add your school name if the order or inventory will be used externally. To add the school name, place the cursor after the last letter in the cell A1 text, press the space bar one time, and type the school name. Press Enter.

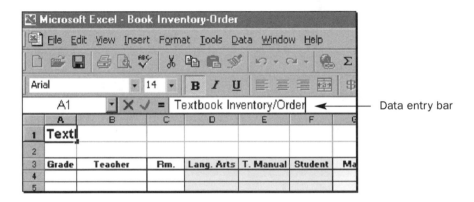

Data entry bar

3 To save the file, click once on File in the menu bar, scroll down to Save As, and click one time. Type a name for the file that will make sense later (e.g., Book Order September 2003–04) and click on the Save button. The file will be saved in the Briefcase Chapter 4 folder on the hard drive. Remember to save the file frequently as you work, but do not rename it.

4 To enter data into the worksheet, place the cursor over a cell (A4 for the first entry) and click once. Type the grade level and press the right arrow key on the keyboard to move to the next cell.

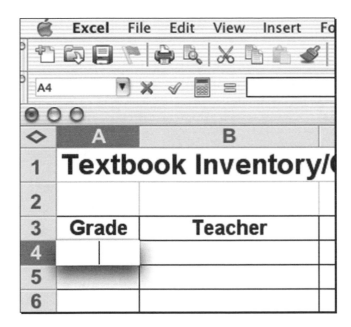

5 Type the teacher's name and press the right arrow key on the keyboard to move to the next cell. Continue entering data in this manner. If a type of textbook (e.g, language arts or math) is not needed, leave the cells blank for book title, teacher's manual, and number of student textbooks and press the right arrow key to move to the next cell where text needs to be entered. When a particular text is needed, type the name of the text in the subject column (e.g., language arts). If a teacher's manual is needed, type 1 in the appropriate column. Enter the number of student texts needed in the Student column.

6 Enter information in subsequent rows, as needed.

 NOTE In some curricular programs, language arts for example, one teacher may need several different textbooks. Enter a complete record for that teacher for each language arts textbook required. (See example below.)

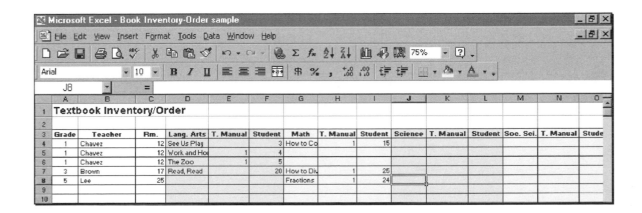

7 Save the file from time to time as you work, but do not rename it.

MANIPULATING THE DATA

In addition to tracking both the current location of books and book orders, the value of this type of file lies in the ability to manipulate data to generate reports quickly.

Three data manipulation techniques are described below: sorting, subtotals, and filtering.

The sample above shows a worksheet that includes a few entries.

Sorting

8 Notice the teacher names are not in alphabetical order. To view names alphabetically, place the cursor over cell B3 (Teacher) and click one time.

9 Click on the Sort Ascending button in the standard toolbar, or click on Data in the menu bar and select Sort. Click OK in the window that appears. The data are now displayed in alphabetical order by teacher name, as shown below:

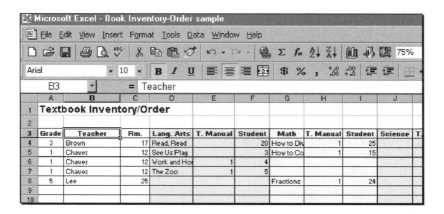

10 To sort alphabetically by teacher name and by book title (e.g., language arts books), place the cursor over B3 and click one time. Click on Data in the menu bar and select Sort. A pop-up window appears. Because the cursor is in B3, the first sort will be by teacher name. Click on the black arrowhead that appears next to the box under "Then by," click and scroll down to Lang. Arts, and click once again. The list is now sorted alphabetically, first by teacher name then by language arts book title.

11 Sorts of this type may be used in any column heading in row 3.

12 To print a sorted report, place the cursor on File, click one time, scroll down to Print, and click OK.

13 Unless new data were entered during the time the file was open, it is not necessary to save before closing.

Subtotals

Subtotals are used with sorted data when values are being tracked. In this inventory/order spreadsheet it is useful to subtotal books in a variety of ways. For example, it's possible to subtotal by grade level the number of teacher manuals and student books ordered for each content area. This feature offers several subtotal options including Sum, Average, and Count.

14 To generate subtotals by grade level, first sort the Grade column in ascending order (see steps 8 and 9).

15 With cell A3 still active, place the cursor on Data in the menu bar, click one time, scroll down and click one time to select Subtotals. A window appears. Make sure Sum is showing in the box headed "Use function." To scroll through the list of options, use the down arrowhead next to the box headed "Add subtotal to." To obtain subtotals for columns titled T. Manual and Student, click the box in front of each of these listings so that a check mark is visible. If a check mark appears anywhere else, click on it to remove it, then click OK.

16 As shown in the sample below, subtotals are now provided for the number of teacher's manuals and student textbooks ordered at each grade level.

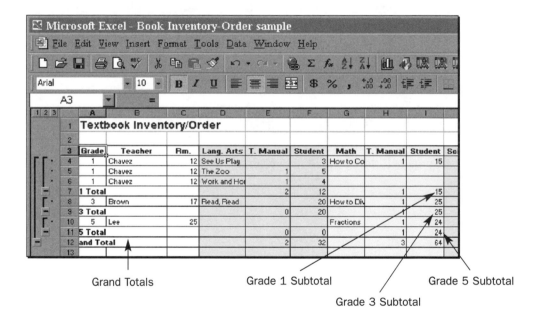

Grand Totals   Grade 1 Subtotal   Grade 5 Subtotal

Grade 3 Subtotal

A variety of other subtotals can be displayed: book title, teacher name, room number, and so on.

17 To print a subtotal report, place the cursor on File, click one time, scroll down to Print, and click OK.

18 To remove subtotals, place the cursor on Data in the menu bar, click one time, scroll down, and click one time to select Subtotals. Then click on Remove All in the window that appears.

19 Unless new data were entered during the time the file was open, it is not necessary to save before closing.

Filtering

Filtering makes it possible to view only those entries that meet certain criteria, for example, entries with math orders only.

20 To use the AutoFilter feature, click on cell A3 and drag to highlight the row through cell O3.

21 Click on Data in the menu bar and scroll down to Filter. A pop-up menu appears. Select and click on AutoFilter.

22 Drop-down boxes with black arrowheads appear in cells A3 through O3. Click on an arrowhead to see a list of all the different kinds of data that appear in the cells in that column. To view only those records with math book orders, click on the arrowhead in the Math column (G), scroll down to NonBlanks, and click one time.

	C	D	E	F	G	H	I	J
1	:ory/Order							
2								
3	Rm ▾	Lang. Ar ▾	T. Manu ▾	Stude ▾	Math ▾	T. Manu ▾	Stude ▾	Scienc ▾
4	17	Read, Read		(All)		1	25	
5	12	See Us Play		(Top 10...)		1	15	
6	12	The Zoo	1	(Custom...) Fractions				
7	12	Work and Hor	1	How to Count				
8	25			How to Divide		1	24	
9				(Blanks)				
10				[NonBlanks]				
11								
12								

23 To see all entries again, select All from the list.

24 You may filter the list setting criteria in any of the columns.

25 To print a filtered report, place the cursor on File, click one time, scroll down to Print, and click OK.

26 To remove the AutoFilter, place the cursor on Data in the menu bar, click and scroll down to Filter. Select and click on AutoFilter in the pop-up menu that appears.

27 Unless new data were entered during the time the file was open, it is not necessary to save before closing.

PRINTING THE WORKSHEET

28 To print the *Book Inventories and Orders* worksheet, click once on File in the menu bar, scroll down to Print, and click OK.

Extensions

Once you are familiar with the template, you may want to

- modify the worksheet further by changing column headings for other content area textbooks you want to track

- use the Insert command on the menu bar to add columns to track textbooks for additional programs

- experiment with combining sorts and filters to generate very specific reports.

Software Inventory

About This Template

Whether software is used in classrooms, a computer lab, or the Library/Media Center, it's important to have an updated inventory that identifies what is available, where it is located, and, in some instances, when its license expires. Unless the site has an automated system that tracks software through bar coding, inventories are often based on physical counts of the programs on hand.

Created in Excel, this template functions as a database that can be used to maintain a current inventory of software found on your campus. Once data are entered for the original inventory, the information can be sorted and filtered by location, grade level, type of program, license expiration date, and so on. Subtotals may also be generated for software titles, types of software, and the like.

SOFTWARE	Excel
ADDITIONAL EQUIPMENT	printer

Template View

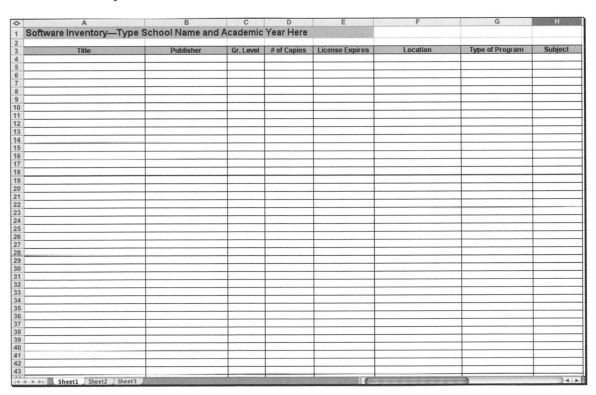

Directions

1 Open the template *Software Inventory* (Software Inventory.xls) found in the Briefcase Chapter 4 folder. (See Getting Started With the Templates in the introduction for directions on opening a template.)

2 Place the cursor over cell A1 and click one time. Notice that the text for cell A1 appears in the data entry bar. Click and drag to highlight the text **Type School Name and Academic Year Here**, then type the information for your school.

3 To enter data into the worksheet, place the cursor over a cell (A4 for the first entry) and click once. Type the name of a software program.

4 Press the right arrow on the keyboard to move the cursor to cell B4. Type the name of the publisher and press the right arrow to move to the next cell.

5 Continue entering information about the software program, including the target grade level(s), the number of copies in this location, the license expiration date (not applicable for all software), and where specifically these copies are located (e.g., the particular classroom, the computer lab, or the Library/Media Center).

6 When you reach columns G (Type of Program) and H (Subject), notice the black arrowhead that appears to the right of the cells.

7 Click once on the arrowhead to see a drop-down list of choices for entries for the cells in these columns.

Scroll down the lists and click on the appropriate choices to enter this information. It's important to enter valid data in these columns so that later searches and filters find all the entries related to a particular type of software program or content area. Using the drop-down list ensures consistency in data entry.

8 Repeat in subsequent rows, as needed. See sample below.

	A	B	C	D	E	F	G	H
1	Software Inventory—Adams Elementary School 2004-05							
2								
3	Title	Publisher	Gr. Level	# of Copies	License Expires	Location	Type of Program	Subject
4	Learning to Count	A Very Good Company	K to 2	3		Room K-1	Drill and Practice	Math
5	Word Processor	The Computer Store	K to 6	1	12/3/04	Room 12	Application	Lang. Arts
6	Apples and Oranges	A Very Good Company	1 to 3	6		Room 5	Problem Solving	Sci.
7	Learning to Count	A Very Good Company	K to 2	1		Computer Lab	Drill and Practice	Math
8								
9								
10								

Sheet1 / Sheet2 / Sheet3

9 To save the file, click once on File in the menu bar, scroll down to Save As, and click one time. Type a name for the file that will make sense later (e.g., Software Inventory 2003–04) and click on the Save button. The file will be saved in the Briefcase Chapter 4 folder on the hard drive. Remember to save the file frequently as you work, but do not rename it.

MODIFYING DATA TYPES

10 If you need to add other types of programs or content areas to the drop-down lists in columns G or H, place the cursor over cell G3 or H3 and click one time. Place the cursor on Data in the menu bar, click once, scroll down to Validation, and click once again.

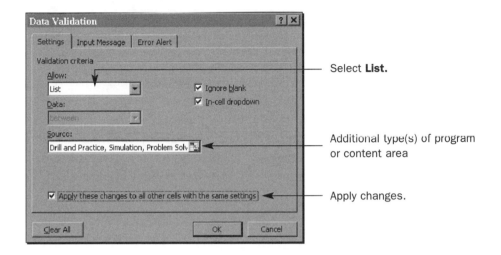

Select **List.**

Additional type(s) of program or content area

Apply changes.

11 Make certain that List is selected under "Allow" (click on the black arrowhead, scroll down to List, and click one time if it is not currently selected).

12 Place the cursor in front of the first word in the box under "Source." Click one time and type the additional type(s) of program or content area. Be sure to add a comma after each new item for the list.

13 Click on the box in front of "Apply these changes to all other cells with the same settings," then click OK.

14 The new items will now appear in the drop-down list.

15 Remember to save the modified worksheet.

MANIPULATING THE DATA

In addition to keeping a list of available software titles, the value of this type of file lies in the ability to manipulate data to generate reports and find software resources quickly.

Three data manipulation techniques are described below: sorting, subtotals, and filtering.

The sample above shows a worksheet that includes a few entries.

Sorting

16 Notice that the software titles are not in alphabetical order. To view titles alphabetically, place the cursor over cell A3 (Title) and click one time.

17 Click on the Sort Ascending button in the standard toolbar, or click on Data in the menu bar and select Sort. Click OK in the window that appears. The data are now displayed in alphabetical order (by title) as shown below:

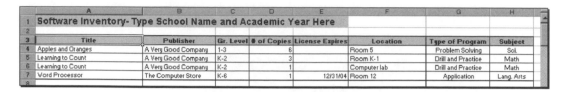

18 To sort alphabetically by title and subject, place the cursor over A3 and click one time. Click on Data in the menu bar and select Sort. A pop-up window appears. Because the cursor is in A3, the first sort will be by title. Click on the black arrow-head that appears next to the box under "Then by," click and scroll down to Type of Program, and click once again. The list is now sorted alphabetically, first by title then by type of program.

19 A sort of this type may be used in any column heading in row 3.

20 To print a sorted report, place the cursor on File, click one time, scroll down to Print, then click OK.

21 Unless new data were entered during the time the file was open, it is not necessary to save before closing.

Subtotals

Subtotals are used with sorted data when values are being tracked. In this software inventory it is useful to subtotal items, such as the number of copies of various software titles. This feature offers several subtotal options, including Sum, Average, and Count.

22 To generate subtotals by number of copies per title, first sort the Title column in ascending order (see steps 16 and 17).

23 With cell A3 still active, place the cursor on Data in the menu bar, click one time, scroll down, then click one time to select Subtotals. A window appears. Make sure Sum is showing in the box headed "Use function." Use the down arrowhead next to the box headed "Add subtotal to" and scroll through the list of options. To obtain subtotals for the number of copies per title, click the box in front of "# of Copies" and a check mark will appear. If a check mark appears anywhere else, click on it to remove it, then click OK.

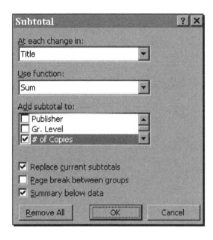

24 As shown in the sample below, subtotals are now provided for the number of copies of each software title.

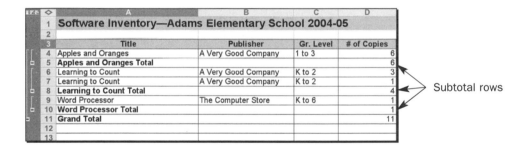

25 A variety of other subtotals can be displayed: publisher, license expirations, locations, and so on.

26 To print a subtotal report, place the cursor on File, click one time, scroll down to Print, and click OK.

27 To remove subtotals, place the cursor on Data in the menu bar, click one time, scroll down, and click one time to select Subtotals. Then click on Remove All in the window that appears.

Filtering

Filtering makes it possible to view only those entries that meet certain criteria, for example, those entries for problem-solving software.

28 To use the AutoFilter feature, click on cell A3 and drag to highlight the row through cell H3.

29 Click on Data in the menu bar and scroll down to Filter. A pop-up menu appears. Select and click on AutoFilter.

30 Drop-down boxes with black arrowheads appear in cells A3 through H3. Cells G3 and H3 will each display two arrowheads when selected because of the data validation feature being used. Click on G3, then on the first arrowhead displayed in this cell. Read the choices given in the drop-down list, which includes all the different kinds of data in cells in column G. To view only the problem-solving software, scroll down to Problem Solving and click one time.

31 To see all entries again, select All from the list.

32 You may filter the list setting criteria in any of the columns.

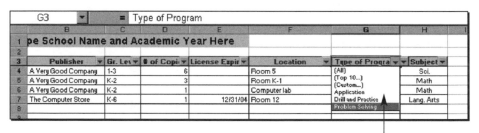

Drop-down menu

33 To remove the AutoFilter, place the cursor on Data in the menu bar, click, and scroll down to Filter. Select and click on AutoFilter in the pop-up menu that appears.

34 To print a filtered report, place the cursor on File, click one time, scroll down to Print, and click OK.

35 Unless new data were entered during the time the file was open, it is not necessary to save before closing.

PRINTING THE WORKSHEET

36 To print the *Software Inventory* worksheet, click once on File in the menu bar, scroll down to Print, and click OK.

Extensions

Once you are familiar with the template, you may want to

- modify the worksheet further by adding columns for other information you want to track. Use the Insert command on the menu bar to add columns.

- experiment with combining sorts and filters to generate very specific reports.

Budget Projection

About This Template

Leveraging resources through multiple funding sources is much easier when you have a tool that enables you to use last year's spending patterns to estimate amounts for each budget category based on next year's allocation.

This template includes five worksheets to track up to five different budget sources. Columns are provided for recording budget categories, a description of each category, and the amounts spent in the categories during the current year. The spreadsheet calculates what percentage of this year's budget was spent in each category and uses this figure and the new allocation to project a figure in each category for next year's budget.

Directions are provided for conducting simple sorts and generating subtotals to examine spending patterns in greater depth. A simple filter technique is also described.

SOFTWARE	Excel
ADDITIONAL EQUIPMENT	printer

Template View

User enters data in these cells.

	A	B	C	D
1	Budget Projection for :	Enter fiscal year		
2				
3	Budget Area:	Enter type of funds, e.g., Title I		
4	This Year's Allocation	$0.00		
5	Next Year's Allocation	$0.00		
6				
7			Total Spent	Allocation for
8	Budget Category	Description	This Year	Next Year
9			$ -	
10			$ -	
11			$ -	
12			$ -	
13			$ -	
14			$ -	
15			$ -	
16			$ -	
17			$ -	
18			$ -	
19			$ -	
20			$ -	

Budget Projection.xls

Budget Projection | Budget Projection (2) | Budget Projection (3) | Budget Projection (4) | Budget Proje

Spreadsheet automatically calculates amounts in cells with green background.

Directions

INITIAL SETUP

1 Open the template *Budget Projection* (Budget Projection.xls) found in the Briefcase Chapter 4 folder. (See Getting Started With the Templates in the introduction for directions on opening a template.)

2 Click on the Budget 1 tab in the lower left corner of the Excel window. Place the cursor over cell B1 and click one time. Type the new fiscal year (for which the projection is being made).

3 Place the cursor over cell B3 and click one time. Type the name of the funding source for this budget, for example, Title I.

4 Place the cursor over cell B4 and click one time. Type this year's total allocation for this budget. Excel will automatically add the dollar sign.

5 Place the cursor over cell B5 and click one time. Type next year's total allocation for this budget. Excel will automatically add the dollar sign.

Click on tabs for Budgets 2–5 to set up the worksheets for each additional funding source. Use the steps above to do this.

For clarity, it is possible to change the name of each worksheet tab to reflect the type of budget on that page.

6 To rename a worksheet tab, right click on the tab.

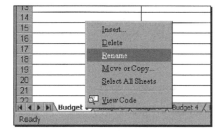

7 Scroll to Rename in the pop-up window that appears, then click one time.

8 The name, Budget 1, is now highlighted. Type the new name, then press Enter.

NOTE Macintosh users change the worksheet tab name by holding down the Control key while clicking the mouse button one time to highlight the name. Then proceed with steps 7 and 8.

INSERTING OR DELETING ROWS

Because of the design of this particular template, it is highly unlikely rows will need to be added or deleted. It is possible to enter information for nearly 100 individual budget categories on each sheet.

MODIFYING HEADINGS

The headings used on these sheets are fairly generic. However, it is possible to customize them for individual district requirements. Each worksheet is protected to avoid accidental overwriting of text and formulas. Here's how to temporarily disable the worksheet protection if necessary.

9 To disable the Protection feature, move the cursor to the lower left corner of the Excel window and click on the tab of the worksheet you want to modify. Place the cursor on Tools in the menu bar, click one time, and scroll down to Protection. A pop-up window appears. Scroll over to Unprotect Sheet and click one time. Repeat this step for each worksheet whose headings will be modified.

10 To change a heading, simply click on the cell where the heading is located and type the new information. Do not attempt to change the information in column D unless you are experienced at writing conditional formulas in Excel.

11 Enable the Protection feature again by repeating Step 9 for each worksheet but selecting the option Protect Sheet that now appears in the pop-up window. Do not enter a password when prompted. Click OK.

12 Save the file by clicking once on File in the menu bar, scrolling down to Save As, and clicking one time. Type a name for the file that will make sense later (e.g., Budget Projection 2004–05) and click on the Save button. The file will be saved in the Briefcase Chapter 4 folder on the hard drive. Remember to save the file frequently as you work, but do not rename it.

USING THE SPREADSHEET TO MAKE PROJECTIONS

13 Move the cursor to the lower left corner of the Excel window and click on the worksheet tab for the budget needed. Position the cursor in cell B9 and click one time. Enter the Budget Category number and click the right arrow. Fill in the Description cell and click the right arrow again. Enter the total amount spent in this category for the current year's budget. Do not type a dollar sign in the column titled Total Spent This Year. Excel will add this automatically and will also calculate a figure for next year's budget based on the amount expended this year and the overall allocation for next year. This figure will appear in the appropriate cell in column D.

14 Place the cursor over the next empty cell in column B and add the description for another budget category. Continue adding data until all budget categories are entered. You now have a projected spending amount for every budget category added.

15 Save the file, but do not rename it.

16 To print a worksheet, click on its tab to make it appear on the screen. Place the cursor on File in the menu bar, click one time, scroll down to Print, then click once again. Click OK in the window that appears.

Extensions

Once you have added data, you can

- recalculate all your projected amounts by entering a new allocation amount in cell B5, based on budget changes

- use Sort and Subtotal features in Excel to create additional reports. Because this is not critical in using this particular template, directions for sorting and generating subtotals are not included here. If you want to try this, disable the sheet protection and refer to directions for the *Book Inventories and Orders* template, also in chapter 4.

Budget Tracking Sheet

About This Template

It's important to track site or departmental expenditures for various budgets, both categorical and general funds. Most districts provide monthly budget reports; however, these can be difficult to interpret and sometimes mistakes are made. By tracking budgets locally, it's possible to compare your reports with those from the main office to ensure clarity and accuracy.

This template includes six worksheets to track up to six different budget sources. Columns are provided for recording budget codes, a description of item(s) purchased, the purchase order number, the cost, and the date ordered. The spreadsheet keeps a running total of expenditures and of funds remaining in the allocation. A column is available for recording when an order arrives.

Directions are provided for conducting simple sorts and generating subtotals to examine spending patterns in greater depth. A simple filter technique is also described for tracking items received.

SOFTWARE	Excel
ADDITIONAL EQUIPMENT	printer

Template View

User enters data in these cells.

Spreadsheet automatically calculates amounts in cells with green background.

◇	A	B	C	D	E	F
1	**Budget Tracking Sheet**					
2						
3	Budget Area:	Enter type of funds, e.g., Title I	Fiscal Year:	Enter year		
4	Total Allocation:		Expended:	$0.00		
5	Carryover:		Balance:	$0.00		
6						
7	**Budget Category**	**Description**	**P.O. Number**	**Amount**	**Date Ordered**	**Received?**
8						
9						
10						
11						
12						
13						
14						
15						
16						
17						
18						
19						
20						
21						
22						
23						

Directions

INITIAL SETUP

1 Open the template *Budget Tracking Sheet* (Budget Tracking Sheet.xls) found in the Briefcase Chapter 4 folder. (See Getting Started With the Templates in the introduction for directions on opening a template.)

2 Click on the Sheet 1 tab in the lower left corner of the Excel window. Place the cursor over cell B3 and click one time. Type the name of the funding source for this budget, for example, Title I.

3 Place the cursor over cell D3 and click one time. Type the current fiscal year, e.g., 2003–04.

4 Place the cursor over cell B4 and click one time. Type the budget allocation. Excel will automatically add the dollar sign. Notice that the amount typed in this cell also appears in cell D5 when Enter is pressed.

5 If this budget has carryover from the previous year, place the cursor over cell B5 and click one time. Type the carryover amount. Excel will automatically add the dollar sign. Notice that when Enter is pressed, the amount entered in cell B5 is now added to the balance displayed in D5.

Sheets 2–6 may be set up using the same steps for other funding sources.

For clarity, it is possible to change the name of each sheet tab to reflect the type of budget on that page.

6 To rename a sheet tab, right click on the tab.

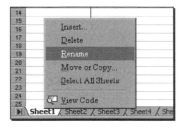

7 Scroll to Rename in the pop-up window that appears, then click one time.

8 The name, Sheet 1, is now highlighted. Type the new name, then press Enter.

 NOTE Macintosh users change the sheet tab name by holding down the Control key while clicking the mouse button one time to highlight the name. Then proceed with steps 7 and 8.

INSERTING OR DELETING ROWS

Because of the design of this particular template, it is highly unlikely rows will need to be added or deleted. It is possible to enter information for 400 individual purchase orders on each sheet.

MODIFYING HEADINGS

The headings used on these sheets are fairly generic. However, it is possible to customize them for individual district requirements. Each sheet is protected to avoid accidental overwriting of text and formulas. Here's how to temporarily disable the sheet protection, if necessary.

9 To disable the Protection feature, click on the tab in the lower left corner of the Excel window for the sheet you want to modify. Place the cursor on Tools in the menu bar, click one time, and scroll down to Protection. A pop-up window appears. Scroll over to Unprotect Sheet, and click one time. Repeat this step for each sheet where headings will be modified.

10 To change a heading, simply click on the cell where the heading is located and type the new information. Do not attempt to change the information in cells D4 and D5 unless you are experienced at writing Excel formulas.

11 Enable the Protection feature again by repeating Step 9 for each sheet but selecting the option Protect Sheet that now appears in the pop-up window. Do not enter a password when prompted. Click OK.

12 Save the file by clicking once on File in the menu bar, scrolling down to Save As, and clicking one time. Type a name for the file that will make sense later (e.g., Budget Tracking Sheet 2003–04) and click on the Save button. The file will be saved in the Briefcase Chapter 4 folder on the hard drive. Remember to save the file frequently as you work, but do not rename it.

ONGOING USE OF THE SPREADSHEET

Each time a purchase order is approved at the site, enter the expenditure information on the appropriate budget sheet. The totals (expended and balance) are automatically calculated. When an ordered item is received, enter a y for Yes in the column titled Received.

13 Click on the sheet tab in the lower left corner of the Excel window for the budget needed. Position the cursor in the first empty cell in the Budget Category column, and click one time. Enter the budget category number and click the right arrow. Fill in the Description cell and click the right arrow again. Continue until the data is entered in the columns titled P.O. Number, Amount, and Date Ordered. (Expenditures such as extra duty for staff and substitute days probably do not have a P.O. number, so leave this cell blank in these cases.) Do not type a dollar sign in the Amount column. Excel will add this automatically and will also calculate the total amount expended to date and the balance. These figures will appear in the appropriate cells in the worksheet.

14 When an ordered item is received, enter a y for Yes in the column titled Received.

15 Save the file.

16 To print a worksheet, click on its tab to make it appear on the screen. Place the cursor on File in the menu bar, click one time, scroll down to Print, then click once again. Click OK in the window that appears.

MANIPULATING THE DATA

In addition to keeping a running total for expenditures, the value of this type of spreadsheet lies in the ability to manipulate data to generate reports and find answers to questions about spending.

Three data manipulation techniques are described below: sorting, filtering, and subtotals.

This sample shows a sheet that includes a few entries:

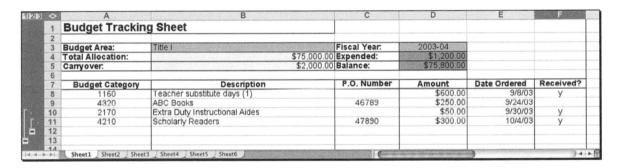

	A	B	C	D	E	F
1	**Budget Tracking Sheet**					
2						
3	**Budget Area:**	Title I	**Fiscal Year:**	2003-04		
4	**Total Allocation:**	$75,000.00	**Expended:**	$1,200.00		
5	**Carryover:**	$2,000.00	**Balance:**	$75,800.00		
6						
7	**Budget Category**	**Description**	**P.O. Number**	**Amount**	**Date Ordered**	**Received?**
8	1160	Teacher substitute days (1)		$600.00	9/8/03	y
9	4320	ABC Books	46789	$250.00	9/24/03	
10	2170	Extra Duty Instructional Aides		$50.00	9/30/03	y
11	4210	Scholarly Readers	47890	$300.00	10/4/03	y
12						
13						
14						

Sheet1 / Sheet2 / Sheet3 / Sheet4 / Sheet5 / Sheet6

Sorting

17 Notice that the budget categories are not in numeric order. To view expenditures in order by budget category, first disable the protection for the sheet (see step 9).

18 Place the cursor over cell A7 (Budget Category) and click one time.

19 Click on the Sort Ascending button in the standard toolbar, or click on Data in the menu bar and select Sort. Click OK in the window that appears. The data are now displayed in numeric order (lowest to highest) as shown below:

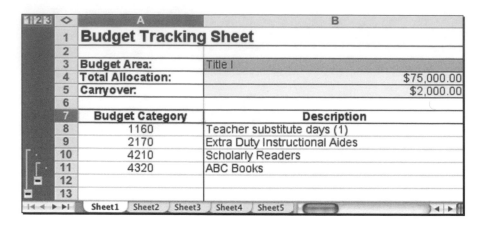

20 A sort of this type may be used in any column heading in row 7.

21 Remember to enable the sheet protection when you are finished (see step 11).

22 Unless new data were entered during the time the file was open, it is not necessary to save before closing.

Subtotals

Subtotals are used with sorted data when values are being tracked. In this budget spreadsheet it is useful to subtotal expenditures by budget category or date. This feature offers several subtotal options, including Sum, Average, and Count.

23 To generate subtotals by Budget Category, first disable the protection for the sheet (see step 9).

24 Sort entries in the Budget Category column in ascending order (see steps 18 and 19).

25 With cell A7 still active, place the cursor on Data in the menu bar, click one time, scroll down and click one time to select Subtotals. A window appears (see below). Make sure Sum is showing in the box headed "Use function" and that Amount is selected in the box headed "Add subtotal to." If a check mark appears anywhere else, click on it to remove it, then click OK.

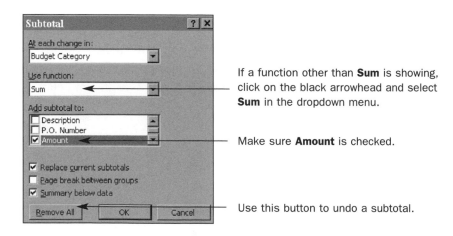

The sheet now displays entries in numeric order by budget category and a subtotal is inserted each time the budget category number changes.

26 To print this sheet view, move the cursor to File, click one time, scroll down to Print, and click OK.

27 To remove the subtotals, click one time on Data, scroll to Subtotals and click one time. Look for the button in the lower left hand corner that says Remove All and click on it (see illustration above).

28 Remember to enable the sheet protection when you are finished (see step 11).

29 Unless new data were entered during the time the file was open, it is not necessary to save before closing.

Filtering

Filtering makes it possible to view only those entries that meet certain criteria, for example, purchases that have been received.

30 To use the AutoFilter feature, first disable the protection for the sheet (see step 9).

31 To execute the AutoFilter function, click on cell A7 and drag to highlight the row through cell F7.

32 Click on Data in the menu bar and scroll down to Filter. A pop-up menu appears. Select and click on AutoFilter.

33 Drop-down boxes with black arrowheads appear in cells A7 through F7. Click on the arrowhead in cell F7 and read the choices given. The list that appears includes all the different kinds of data in cells in column F.

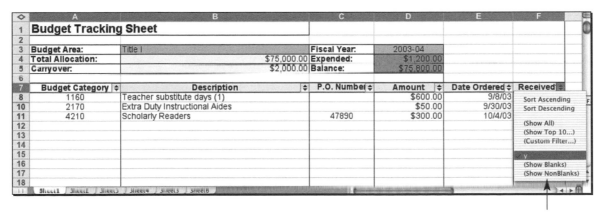

Drop-down menu

34 To view only the entries marked y (meaning they have been received), scroll down to y and click one time.

35 To view only the entries that have not been received, choose Show Blanks from the list.

36 To see all entries again, select Show All from the list.

37 To remove the AutoFilter, place the cursor on Data in the menu bar, click, and scroll down to Filter. Select and click on AutoFilter in the pop-up menu that appears.

38 Remember to enable the sheet protection when you are finished (see step 11).

39 Unless new data were entered during the time the file was open, it is not necessary to save before closing.

PRINTING THE SHEET

40 To print the *Budget Tracking Sheet*, click once on File in the menu bar, scroll down to Print, and click OK.

Extensions

Once you have customized the template and added data, you might also want to

- practice sorts, filters, and subtotals using different columns of data

- experiment with combining sorts, filters, and subtotals to generate very specific reports.

Classroom/Department Expenditures Form

About This Template

Sites often allocate budgets for individual classrooms or grade levels (elementary) and for departments (secondary and district office).

Use this template throughout the school year to track monthly expenditures for these groups. Separate worksheets are provided for each of the two semesters, and annual totals are automatically calculated on a third worksheet. The worksheets are safeguarded by the software's Protection feature to prevent accidentally changing formulas during data entry.

Directions are also provided for generating simple clustered column charts to represent expenditures graphically. Begin by identifying an annual budget for each group, then add expended amounts on an ongoing basis.

SOFTWARE	Excel
ADDITIONAL EQUIPMENT	printer

Template View

SEMESTER 1 WORKSHEET

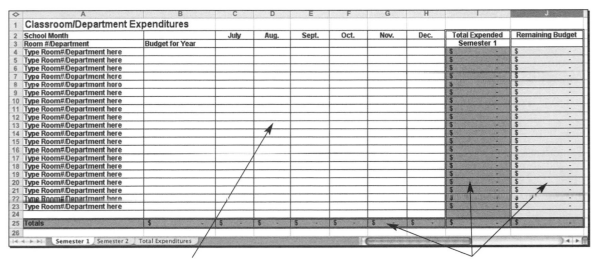

Data are entered in these cells in columns A through H.

Spreadsheet automatically calculates amounts in cells with shaded backgrounds.

SEMESTER 2 WORKSHEET

	A	B	C	D	E	F	G	H	I	J	K
1	Classroom/Department Expenditures										
2	School Month		Jan.	Feb.	Mar.	Apr.	May	June	Total Expended Semester 2	Remaining Budget	
3	Room #/Department	Budget for Year									
4	Type Room#/Department here	$ -							$ -	$ -	
5	Type Room#/Department here	$ -							$ -	$ -	
6	Type Room#/Department here	$ -							$ -	$ -	
7	Type Room#/Department here	$ -							$ -	$ -	
8	Type Room#/Department here	$ -							$ -	$ -	
9	Type Room#/Department here	$ -							$ -	$ -	
10	Type Room#/Department here	$ -							$ -	$ -	
11	Type Room#/Department here	$ -							$ -	$ -	
12	Type Room#/Department here	$ -							$ -	$ -	
13	Type Room#/Department here	$ -							$ -	$ -	
14	Type Room#/Department here	$ -							$ -	$ -	
15	Type Room#/Department here	$ -							$ -	$ -	
16	Type Room#/Department here	$ -							$ -	$ -	
17	Type Room#/Department here	$ -							$ -	$ -	
18	Type Room#/Department here	$ -							$ -	$ -	
19	Type Room#/Department here	$ -							$ -	$ -	
20	Type Room#/Department here	$ -							$ -	$ -	
21	Type Room#/Department here	$ -							$ -	$ -	
22	Type Room#/Department here	$ -							$ -	$ -	
23	Type Room#/Department here	$ -							$ -	$ -	
24											
25	Total Budgeted	$ -	$ -	$ -	$ -	$ -	$ -	$ -	$ -	$ -	
26											

Semester 1 | Semester 2 | Total Expenditures

Spreadsheet automatically adds values from Semester 1 worksheet.

Data are entered in these cells in columns C through H.

Spreadsheet automatically calculates amounts in cells with shaded backgrounds.

TOTAL EXPENDITURES WORKSHEET

	A	B	C	D
1	Classroom/Department Expenditures			
2	Annual Totals			
3	Room #/Department	Budget for Year	Total Expended	Remaining Budget
4	Type Room#/Department here	$ -	$ -	$ -
5	Type Room#/Department here	$ -	$ -	$ -
6	Type Room#/Department here	$ -	$ -	$ -
7	Type Room#/Department here	$ -	$ -	$ -
8	Type Room#/Department here	$ -	$ -	$ -
9	Type Room#/Department here	$ -	$ -	$ -
10	Type Room#/Department here	$ -	$ -	$ -
11	Type Room#/Department here	$ -	$ -	$ -
12	Type Room#/Department here	$ -	$ -	$ -
13	Type Room#/Department here	$ -	$ -	$ -
14	Type Room#/Department here	$ -	$ -	$ -
15	Type Room#/Department here	$ -	$ -	$ -
16	Type Room#/Department here	$ -	$ -	$ -
17	Type Room#/Department here	$ -	$ -	$ -
18	Type Room#/Department here	$ -	$ -	$ -
19	Type Room#/Department here	$ -	$ -	$ -
20	Type Room#/Department here	$ -	$ -	$ -
21	Type Room#/Department here	$ -	$ -	$ -
22	Type Room#/Department here	$ -	$ -	$ -
23	Type Room#/Department here	$ -	$ -	$ -
24				
25	Totals	$ -	$ -	$ -
26				

Semester 1 | Semester 2 | Total Expenditures

All values for cells in this worksheet are automatically inserted from Semester 1 and Semester 2 worksheets.

Directions

INITIAL SETUP

1 Open the template *Classroom/Department Expenditures* (Classroom-Department Expend.xls) found in the Briefcase Chapter 4 folder. (See Getting Started With the Templates in the introduction for directions on opening a template.)

2 Click on the Semester 1 tab in the lower left corner of the Excel window. Place the cursor over cell A4 and click one time. Type the first room number, grade level, or department name. To enter the next room number, grade level, or department name, press the down arrow on the keyboard, then type the information. Continue until each room, grade level, or department that has a separate budget is included in the list.

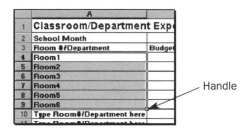 Handle

 NOTE If the list of room numbers or grade levels to be added is sequential (as shown in the example), type the first entry. Notice the handle that appears in the lower right corner of the cell. Place the cursor over the handle and click and drag this handle down the cells in the column. Room numbers will appear sequentially in the cells you highlight.

INSERTING OR DELETING ROWS

The template has 20 rows. If additional rows are needed, they may be added, but the Protection feature that prevents users from overwriting formulas that automatically add data to the shaded cells must be temporarily disabled. This is also necessary if there are too many rows and some need to be deleted.

3 To disable the Protection feature, click on the Semester 1 tab in the lower left corner of the Excel window. Place the cursor on Tools in the menu bar, click one time, and scroll down to Protection. A pop-up window appears. Scroll over to Unprotect Sheet, and click one time. Repeat this step for the Semester 2 and Total Expenditures worksheets.

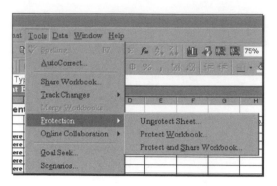

4 To insert rows, hold down the Shift key and click on each tab in the lower left corner of the window (Semester 1, Semester 2, and Total Expenditures). By doing this, extra rows added to the Semester 1 worksheet are also inserted in the Semester 2 and Total Expenditures worksheets. Place the cursor over cell A23 and click one time. Place the cursor on Insert in the menu bar, click one time, and scroll to Rows. Click one time. Repeat as needed. Using this technique duplicates formatting. To duplicate formulas, click and drag to highlight the cells in the row just above the newly inserted rows. Position the cursor over the handle that appears in the lower right corner of the highlighted row. Click and drag this handle down until the new row(s) are highlighted. (See *Note* above.)

5 To delete unneeded rows, hold down the Shift key and click on each tab in the lower left corner of the window (Semester 1, Semester 2, and Total Expenditures). By doing this, extra rows in each worksheet are simultaneously deleted. Click and drag down through the numbers of the extra rows, along the left side of the worksheet, to highlight the rows. With the rows highlighted, place the cursor on Edit in the menu bar, click one time, scroll down to Delete, and click once again. The highlighted rows are now deleted.

6 Enable the Protection feature again by repeating step 3 for each worksheet but selecting the option Protect Sheet that now appears in the pop-up window. Select this option for each worksheet. Do not enter a password when prompted. Click OK.

7 To add the annual budget amount for each classroom, grade level, or department, begin by placing the cursor over cell B4 and clicking one time. Type the budget figure for the first entry. A dollar sign will be automatically added. Press the down arrow on the keyboard and type the amount for the second listing. Repeat this step until all budget amounts are added. The template file is designed to automatically add this information to the other two worksheets.

8 Save the file by clicking once on File in the menu bar, scrolling down to Save As, and clicking one time. Type a name for the file that will make sense later (e.g., My School Classroom Expenditures 2003–04) and click on the Save button. The file will be saved in the Briefcase Chapter 4 folder on the hard drive. Remember to save the file frequently as you work, but do not rename the file.

ONGOING USE OF THE SPREADSHEET

Every month, enter the amount spent for the month for each classroom, grade level, or department. The months July through December are listed on the Semester 1 worksheet, and the months January through June are listed on the Semester 2 worksheet. Other totals (overall expenditures and remaining budget) are automatically calculated.

9 Position the cursor in row 4 of the column for the current month, click one time, then type the amount. Press the down arrow on the keyboard to move to the next cell for that month. Do not type a dollar sign. Excel will add this automatically and will also automatically calculate the total amount spent to date and the amount remaining for each classroom, grade level, or department. These figures will appear in the appropriate cells in each worksheet.

10 To print a worksheet, click on its tab to make it appear on the screen. Place the cursor on File in the menu bar, click one time, scroll down to Print, then click once again. Click OK in the window that appears.

CREATING A SIMPLE CLUSTERED COLUMN CHART

Charts contain one or more data series. A data series consists of a set of numbers related to a specific category. For example, in this template, expenditures for Room 1 comprise a data series, as do expenditures for the month of July.

Charts have an x-axis (horizontal) and a y-axis (vertical). They may include titles and legends.

Excel has a Chart Wizard, a useful tool that leads you through the steps for building a chart.

This example shows how to create a chart for expenditures in Rooms 1–3 for July through September.

11 Disable the sheet protection (see step 3 above).

12 Click on the Semester 1 tab in the lower left corner of the window. Place the cursor in C4. Click and drag right and down to highlight through cell E6. This identifies the data series to be used in the chart.

 13 Click on the Chart Wizard button in the standard toolbar, or click on Insert in the menu bar and select Chart. This is the dialog box that appears:

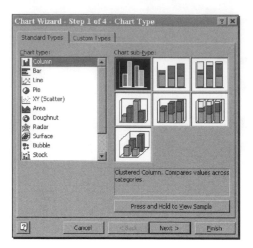

14 The default selection is a Clustered Column. To compare values across categories, click Next.

15 This dialog box shows how the data will be displayed when the series is arranged by rows.

16 While still looking at the Step 2 dialog box, click on the Series tab. To label each data series, change the listings Series 1–3 to Room 1, Room 2, and Room 3 by clicking on a listing and typing the correct label. For example, click on the listing Series 1 and type Room 1 in the Name box.

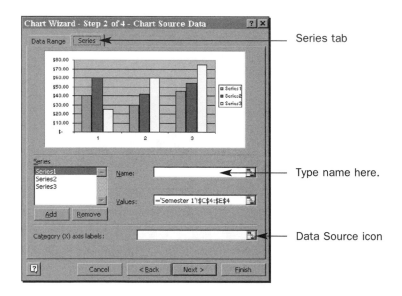

17 To identify the labels for the x-axis, click on the Data Source icon in the box on the right of where it reads "Category (X) axis labels."

18 Now the Semester 1 worksheet is visible. Click and drag across cells C2 through E2. Click on the Close box in the Chart Source Data toolbar (see below).

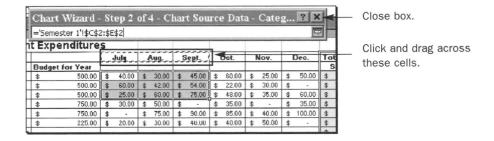

Close box.

Click and drag across these cells.

19 Click Next.

20 Type Expenditures Rooms 1–3 in the Chart Title box. Click Next.

21 Click on the Radio button next to "As new sheet," and type 1st Quarter Rooms 1–3. Click Finish.

22 The chart now appears on a new sheet, and there is a new sheet tab called 1st Quarter Rooms 1–3 in the lower left corner of the window.

23 To print a chart, click on its tab to make it appear on the screen. Place the cursor on File in the menu bar, click one time, scroll down to Print, then click once again. Click on OK in the window that appears.

24 To include a chart in a Word document, click anywhere in the chart to make it active. Place the cursor on Edit in the menu bar, scroll down to Copy, and click one time. Open the Word document, place the cursor where you want the chart to go (remember to click one time when the cursor is positioned), place the cursor on Edit in the menu bar, scroll down to Paste, and click one time.

25 When you are finished, enable the Protection feature again by repeating step 3 but clicking on Protect Sheet in the pop-up window. Do this for each worksheet. Do not enter a password when prompted. Click OK.

Extensions

Once you have customized the template and added data, you might also want to

- experiment using different kinds of charts in the Chart Wizard

- generate a chart that compares noncontiguous data series, for example, one that compares Room 4 and Room 6 expenditures. Highlight the cells from Rooms 4 through 6. On the second step in the Chart Wizard, click on the Series tab; three series are currently listed. Click on the series you do not want to use, then click on Remove. The chart will show data for the remaining series (Rooms 4 and 6).

CHAPTER FIVE

Assessment and Evaluation

V. Assessment and Evaluation

Educational leaders use technology to plan and implement comprehensive systems of effective assessment and evaluation. Educational leaders:

   A use multiple methods to assess and evaluate appropriate uses of technology resources for learning, communication, and productivity.

   B use technology to collect and analyze data, interpret results, and communicate findings to improve instructional practice and student learning.

   C assess staff knowledge, skills, and performance in using technology and use results to facilitate quality professional development and to inform personnel decisions.

   D use technology to assess, evaluate, and manage administrative and operational systems.

The briefcase contains three word processing templates and two spreadsheet templates related to NETS•A V. The chart below lists the templates included in this chapter and indicates the correlation between each template and one or more Standard V performance indicators provided above. In this case, all four performance indicators are supported.

TEMPLATE	PROGRAM	NETS•A V PERFORMANCE INDICATORS			
		V.A.	V.B.	V.C.	V.D.
Evaluation Planning Chart	Word	●			
Evaluation Rubric	Word	●			
Staff Survey Form	Word	●	●	●	●
Staff Survey Results	Excel	●	●	●	●
Standardized Test Scores	Excel		●		

Evaluation Planning Chart

About This Template

Assessment and accountability are key terms in education today. The No Child Left Behind Act requires that programs be monitored and reviewed on a regular basis. Designing an evaluation plan is a daunting task for some, but steps can be taken to make plan design more manageable. It's best to do this work while the program itself is being developed, but later is better than never.

Use this template to scrutinize the program goals. Ask, "Why are we writing this goal, and what outcome are we anticipating? How will we know when we are successful? What information sources do we have for data collection, and what benchmarks will show progress?" The template provides areas to answer each question. It may be used in conjunction with the *Evaluation Plan Overview* template (chapter 1) and the *Evaluation Rubric* template (chapter 5).

SOFTWARE	Word
ADDITIONAL EQUIPMENT	printer

Template View

Evaluation Planning Chart for Type Name of Program Here

Goal: Highlight this text and type the goal here.

What do we want to know?	What would success look like?	What sources of information can we use?	What are our benchmarks?
Sample question: How has student achievement improved through use of handheld computers in science classes? (Highlight the text in this area and enter your own text here.)	Sample descriptor: Students using handheld computers in science classes increase the amount and quality of data collected in lab exercises. (Highlight the text in this area and enter your own text here.)	Sample sources: Student lab reports, teacher observation. (Highlight the text in this area and enter your own text here.)	Sample benchmark: By the end of first semester, all students participating in the pilot program will have completed three labs using handhelds, with a score of 80% or better on data collection. (Highlight the text in this area and enter your own text here.)

Directions

1 Open the template *Evaluation Planning Chart* (Evaluation Planning Chart.doc) found in the Briefcase Chapter 5 folder. (See Getting Started With the Templates in the introduction for directions on opening a template.)

2 Click on View in the menu bar. Scroll down to Header and Footer and click one time. In the header, double-click on the first word in **Type Name of Program Here** to highlight the field, then type the name of the program being considered. For example, Handheld Computers in Science, or Early Literacy. Click on Close in the Header and Footer toolbar.

3 To save the file, click once on File in the menu bar, scroll down to Save As, and click one time. Type a name for the file that will make sense later (e.g., Evaluation Planning Chart—Handhelds), and click on the Save button.

4 Enter the answer to each question in the space provided by clicking and dragging the cursor on the text in each answer area, then typing a response. The answer area in the first table includes sample responses. Because this form is a table, the answer area will expand automatically if additional space is needed.

5 Depending on the outcomes identified, a goal area may require more than one question in the "What do we want to know?" column. If additional rows for other questions are needed, place the cursor on the last row and click one time.

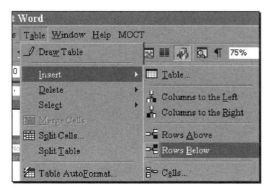

6 Click once on Table in the menu bar, scroll down to Insert and click on Rows Below, which appears in the pop-up window. Repeat as needed.

7 Save the file from time to time (do not rename the file again).

ADDING OR DELETING TABLES

The template includes tables for five goals.

8 If you need additional tables, click inside any existing table. Place the cursor on Table in the menu bar, click one time, and scroll down to Select. Drag the cursor over to Table in the pop-up window that appears, and click on Table. The table will be highlighted.

9 Place the cursor on Edit in the menu bar, click one time, and scroll down to Copy. Click one time.

10 Move the cursor to the place where you want to insert the new table, and click one time.

11 Place the cursor on Edit in the menu bar, click one time, and scroll down to Paste. Click one time. A new table will appear in the document.

12 To delete an unneeded table, click inside the table you want to delete. Place the cursor on Table in the menu bar, click one time, and scroll down to Delete. Drag the cursor over to Table in the pop-up window that appears, and click on Table. The table will be deleted.

PRINTING THE CHART

13 To print the planning chart, click once on File in the menu bar, scroll down to Print, and click OK.

Extensions

Once you have answered the questions in the template, you might want to use either the Highlight or Font Color features on the formatting toolbar to emphasize key words and phrases in your responses or to visually categorize various types of information sources or benchmark dates.

Evaluation Rubric

About This Template

Once evaluation questions are identified (see the template *Evaluation Planning Chart* in this chapter), along with descriptors for success, sources of data, and benchmarks, it's helpful to have an organizer that puts this information into rubric form for evaluation and monitoring.

Use this template both to identify the specific changes you expect to see, based on program goals and outcomes, and to describe criteria for early, partial, and full implementation of a goal. Space is also provided for implementation dates and comments. This template may also be used in conjunction with the *Evaluation Plan Overview* template (chapter 1).

SOFTWARE	Word
ADDITIONAL EQUIPMENT	printer

Template View

Evaluation Rubric for Type Name of Program Here

Goal: Type a goal statement here.

There is evidence that:

A. Type an outcome statement here.

Implementation dates: Type the beginning and ending dates here.		
1	2	3
Highlight this text and enter descriptors for early stages of implementation of the outcome.	Highlight this text and enter descriptors for partial implementation of the outcome.	Highlight this text and enter descriptors for full implementation of the outcome.
Comments:		

Directions

1 Open the template *Evaluation Rubric* (Evaluation Rubric.doc) found in the Briefcase Chapter 5 folder. (See Getting Started With the Templates in the introduction for directions on opening a template.)

2 Click on View in the menu bar. Scroll down to Header and Footer and click one time. In the header, double-click on the first word in **Type Name of Program Here** to highlight the field, then type the name of the program being considered, for example, Handheld Computers in Science, or Early Literacy. Click on Close in the Header and Footer toolbar.

3 The template is designed for one goal with up to four evaluation outcomes. The easiest way to work with multiple goals is to open and save a new file for each goal area. If a goal has fewer than four evaluation outcomes, tables may be deleted. If a table has more than four evaluation outcomes, tables may be added. See Adding and Deleting Tables below.

4 To save the file, click once on File in the menu bar, scroll down to Save As, and click one time. Type a name for the file that will make sense later (e.g., Evaluation Rubric: Handhelds—Goal 1) and click on the Save button.

5 Double-click on the first word in **Type a goal statement here** to highlight the field, then type a program goal. Press Tab to move to the next field.

6 Pressing Tab highlights the field. You may also double-click on the first word in **Type an outcome statement here** to highlight the field, then type the expected outcome. If you have completed the *Evaluation Planning Chart* template found in this chapter, use the questions generated in those tables. Press Tab to move to the next field.

7 Pressing Tab highlights the field. You may also double-click on the first word in **Type the beginning and ending dates here** to highlight the field, then type the dates.

8 This three-point rubric requires descriptors for early, partial, and full implementation. If you have completed the *Evaluation Planning Chart* template found in this chapter, use the descriptors, data sources, and benchmarks generated in those tables to write the descriptors. Because this form is a table, the response area will expand automatically if additional space is needed.

9 Save the file from time to time (do not rename the file again).

10 Repeat steps 1 through 9 for remaining goals.

ADDING AND DELETING TABLES

As mentioned previously, the template is designed for one goal with up to four evaluation outcomes.

11 If you need additional outcome areas, click and drag to highlight the text and table as shown below.

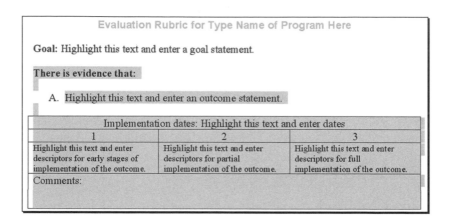

12 Place the cursor on Edit in the menu bar, click one time, and scroll down to Copy. Click one time.

13 Move the cursor to the end of the document and click one time.

14 Place the cursor on Edit in the menu bar, click one time, and scroll down to Paste. Click one time. An outcome area will appear at the end of the document.

15 To delete extra outcome areas, highlight the unneeded outcome area as shown above. Place the cursor on Edit in the menu bar, click one time, and scroll down to Cut. Click one time. The extra area is now deleted. Repeat as needed.

USING THE RUBRIC

16 Once the rubric is completed for each goal and outcome area, print and distribute copies to those involved in monitoring and evaluation. You may also distribute copies of the files for recording-keeping purposes. For example, at the end of the evaluation period, mark each score by highlighting the appropriate number and typing Control-U to underline the score (Command-U for Macintosh users). Comments about each area may be added in the space provided in the table.

17 Save modified files for the evaluation report.

PRINTING THE RUBRIC

18 To print the rubric, click once on File in the menu bar, scroll down to Print, and click OK.

Extensions

While setting up the original rubric, you may want to

- experiment with the Copy, Paste, and Cut features to incorporate all goals and outcome areas into one file

- use the Table Properties feature to shade the cell with the appropriate rubric score.

Staff Survey Form

About This Template

Whether you need to evaluate an instructional program, ask staff to self-assess their technology skills, or monitor implementation of a new management system, a survey is an efficient method for gathering data from a large number of people.

This template uses the Forms feature in Word to help you create a survey form quickly that will be specific to your needs. Text is entered in the shaded fields. The remaining text is protected unless you disable a feature called Protect Form. Directions for disabling this protection are provided.

This template may be used in conjunction with the *Staff Survey Results* template, also found in this chapter.

SOFTWARE	Word
ADDITIONAL EQUIPMENT	printer

Template View

| Enter School or District Name Here |
| Enter Name of Survey Here |

This survey is part of an evaluation of the enter name of program here program. Your responses will be reported anonymously.

Please respond to each of the following items by marking the box for the answer that most closely reflects your experience with the enter name of program here program. The rating scale is explained below.

4 = Often 3 = Occasionally 2 = Seldom 1 = Never	4	3	2	1
Item 1				
Item 2				
Item 3				
Item 4				
Item 5				
Item 6				
Item 7				
Item 8				
Item 9				
Item 10				
Item 11				
Item 12				
Item 13				
Item 14				
Item 15				
Item 16				
Item 17				
Item 18				
Item 19				
Item 20				

Please mark your current position:

☐ Teacher　　☐ Administrator　　☐ Paraprofessional

☐ Support Staff　　☐ Other

Comments:

Thank you for taking the time to complete this survey. Your input is important in planning and monitoring our instructional programs. Please return this survey to enter name by date.

Directions

1　Open the *Staff Survey Form* template (Staff Survey Form.doc) found in the Briefcase Chapter 5 folder. (See Getting Started With the Templates in the introduction for directions on opening a template.)

2 Double-click on the first word in the text **Enter School or District Name Here** to highlight the field, then type the school or district name. Press Tab to move to the next field.

3 Pressing Tab highlights the field. You may also double-click on the first word in the text **Enter Name of Survey Here** to highlight the field, then type the name of the survey (e.g., Self-Assessment of Technology Integration Skills). Press Tab to move to the next field.

4 Pressing Tab highlights the field. You may also double-click on the first word in the text **enter name of program here** to highlight the field, then type the name of the program being evaluated (e.g., Teachers and Technology Integration). Press Tab to move to the next field.

5 The next field requires the same information as step 4.

6 The next four fields contain descriptors for the 4-point rating scale. If these descriptors are appropriate, tab through them without making any changes. If the descriptors need to be changed, press Tab to highlight each field and make changes.

7 Press Tab or double-click on the first word in the text Item 1 to highlight the field, then type the first survey item. Press Tab to move to the next field. Continue adding Items 2–20. The fields will expand to accommodate all text entered.

8 The form includes space for 20 survey items. If you need more than 20 items or have fewer than 20 items, first disable the form protection by placing the cursor on View in the menu bar, clicking one time, scrolling down to Toolbars, and selecting Forms from the pop-up window.

Padlock

9 Click one time on the icon that looks like a padlock.

10 To insert additional rows, click in the row for Item 20. Place the cursor on Table in the menu bar. Click one time, scroll down to Insert, and click on Rows Below in the pop-up window that appears. Repeat until you have inserted the number of rows needed. Type the additional survey items.

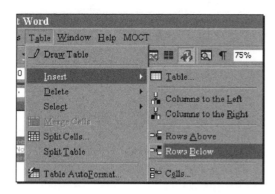

11 To delete unneeded rows, click and drag to highlight the extra rows. Place the cursor on Table in the menu bar. Click one time, scroll down to Delete, and click on Rows.

12 Enable the form protection again by repeating steps 8 and 9.

13 Tab through the boxes for marking staff positions. Add appropriate text to the final two shaded fields by double-clicking on **enter name** and **date**, identifying who is collecting surveys and when they are due.

14 To save the file, click once on File in the menu bar, scroll down to Save As, and click one time. Type a name for the file that will make sense later (e.g., Staff Survey Form—Technology Integration Skills) and click on the Save button. The file will be saved in the Briefcase Chapter 5 folder on the hard drive. Remember to save the file frequently while you work, but do not rename the file.

PRINTING THE STAFF SURVEY FORM

15 To print the survey for distribution, click once on File in the menu bar, scroll down to Print, and click OK. The shading in the fields does not appear when the document is printed.

Extensions

Once you have used this template to create a staff survey, you might want to

- modify the form to use with students or parents. Remember to disable the form protection before attempting to make changes.

- experiment with adding or deleting rating scale columns for a 3- or 5-point survey.

Staff Survey Results

About This Template

Distributing a survey is easy, but then the results need to be tallied and analyzed. Some districts and schools have software and scanning devices to do this data analysis and review. However, if your district does not have this capability, or if it's not practical to use it for a small, local survey, then this template can be used in conjunction with the *Staff Survey Form* template, also found in this chapter.

This template includes two worksheets, one for data entry and the other to automatically generate a report of results. The Survey Data worksheet is currently set up to handle 75 surveys consisting of up to 20 questions, but additional rows may be added for more surveys.

SOFTWARE	Excel
ADDITIONAL EQUIPMENT	printer

Template View

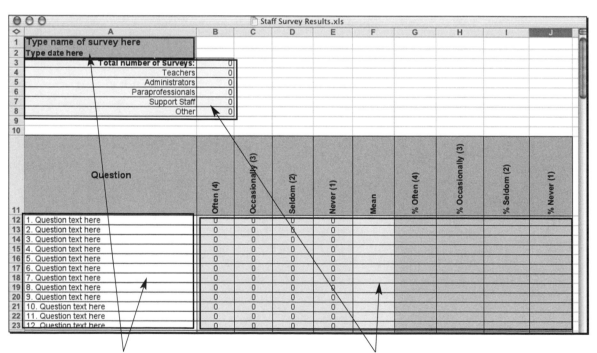

User enters data in these cells.

Spreadsheet automatically enters data
from Survey Data sheet into these cells.

SURVEY REPORT TAB

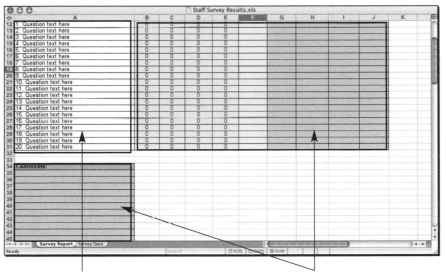

User enters data in these cells.

Spreadsheet automatically enters data from Survey Data sheet into these cells.

SURVEY DATA TAB

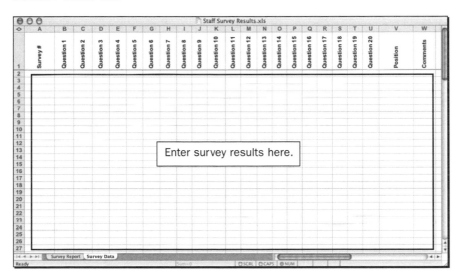

Sums, counts, and means are automatically calculated and placed into the Survey Report worksheet.

Directions

INITIAL SETUP FOR SURVEY REPORT TAB

1 Open the template *Staff Survey Results* (Staff Survey Results.xls) found in the Briefcase Chapter 5 folder. (See Getting Started With the Templates in the introduction for directions on opening a template.)

2 Click on the Survey Report tab in the lower left corner of the Excel window. Place the cursor on cell A1 and click one time. Type the name of the survey, for example, Language Arts Program.

3 Place the cursor on cell A2 and click one time. Type the date for the survey, for example, October 2003.

4 Place the cursor on cell A12, click and drag to highlight the text "Question text here," and type the text for the first survey question. Use this technique for all survey questions. If you need to widen column A, disable the Protection feature, place the cursor on the column heading row between columns A and B, and click and drag the mouse to the right.

5 To disable the Protection feature, place the cursor on Tools in the menu bar, click one time, and scroll down to Protection. A pop-up window appears. Scroll over to Unprotect Sheet, and click one time. Make needed changes.

6 Enable the Protection feature again by repeating step 5 but choosing the option Protect Sheet that now appears in the pop-up window. Select this option for each worksheet. Do not enter a password when prompted. Click OK.

7 If you have fewer than 20 questions, you may delete the extra rows. Disable the Protection feature (see step 5). Click and drag to highlight the rows to delete. Place the cursor on Edit in the menu bar, click one time, then scroll down to Delete and click. Select Entire row in the pop-up window and click OK. Remember to enable the Protection feature again when you are finished (see step 6).

8 Notice that the current responses for the Likert Scale ratings are: Often, Occasionally, Seldom, and Never. If these responses are not appropriate for this survey, you can change them by disabling the Protection feature, clicking on each cell, and typing the new responses. Don't forget to enable the Protection feature when you finish.

9 Save the file by clicking once on File in the menu bar, scrolling down to Save As, and clicking one time. Type a name for the file that will make sense later (e.g., Language Arts Program Survey Results 10-03) and click on the Save button. The file will be saved in the Briefcase Chapter 5 folder on the hard drive. Remember to save the file frequently as you work, but do not rename it.

INITIAL SETUP FOR SURVEY DATA TAB

This worksheet is formatted for up to 75 surveys with up to 20 questions. If data must be entered for additional surveys, more rows may be inserted. No additional setup is needed for this worksheet prior to entering data.

INSERTING ROWS

To tabulate more than 75 surveys, additional rows must be inserted. You do not need to delete extra rows if fewer than 75 surveys are being tabulated. Follow the steps below to add additional rows:

10 The worksheet is protected to preserve the formulas needed. To disable the Protection feature, place the cursor on Tools in the menu bar, click one time, and scroll down to Protection. A pop-up window appears. Scroll over to Unprotect Sheet, and click one time.

11 To insert a new row or multiple new rows, place the cursor in any cell in rows 2 through 76 in column A, and click one time. Place the cursor on Insert in the menu bar, click one time, scroll down to Rows, and click once again. Repeat to add the number of new rows required.

12 Enable the Protection feature again by repeating step 5 but choosing the option Protect Sheet that now appears in the pop-up window. Select this option for each worksheet. Do not enter a password when prompted. Click OK.

13 Save the file. It is not necessary to rename the file again.

ENTERING DATA

After a staff survey has been distributed and collected, use the Survey Data worksheet for data entry.

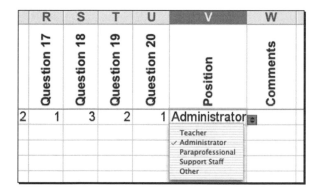

14 Click on the Survey Data tab in the lower left corner of the Excel window. Position the cursor in the first empty cell in the Survey # column (A2 when just getting started), and click one time. Enter an identification number for the first survey. The identification number may be sequential numbering from 1–75 or whatever other system you'd like to use. The purpose of the number is so you can track the total number of surveys tabulated and to help you locate a specific survey when you might need to check the accuracy of data entered. Click the right arrow to move to column B.

15 Enter the score for the first question (1–4) and press the right arrow to move to column C. Continue entering the score for each question through Question 20.

16 Column V is used to identify the position held by the respondent. Click on the black arrowhead that appears in the upper right corner of the cell and scroll down to select the appropriate title. Click to enter the selection into the cell.

17 Column W is used to record any handwritten comments on the survey form. Click on the appropriate cell in this column and type the comment as written on the survey. Do not worry if you cannot see the entire comment after it's typed and Enter is pressed. The full comment will appear on the Survey Report worksheet in the Comments section.

18 Repeat steps 14–17 for each survey. Remember to save the file periodically, but do not rename it.

VIEWING THE RESULTS

As data is entered on the Survey Data worksheet, the results are automatically tabulated and entered into the Survey Report worksheet (see below).

19 To review the tabulation, click on the Survey Report tab.

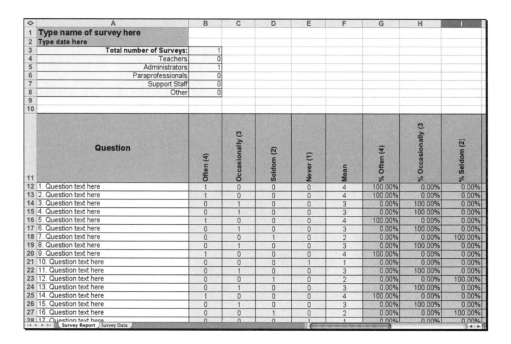

	A	B	C	D	E	F	G	H	I
1	Type name of survey here								
2	Type date here								
3	Total number of Surveys:	1							
4	Teachers	0							
5	Administrators	1							
6	Paraprofessionals	0							
7	Support Staff	0							
8	Other	0							
9									
10									
11	Question	Often (4)	Occasionally (3	Seldom (2)	Never (1)	Mean	% Often (4)	% Occasionally (3	% Seldom (2)
12	1. Question text here	1	0	0	0	4	100.00%	0.00%	0.00%
13	2. Question text here	1	0	0	0	4	100.00%	0.00%	0.00%
14	3. Question text here	0	1	0	0	3	0.00%	100.00%	0.00%
15	4. Question text here	0	1	0	0	3	0.00%	100.00%	0.00%
16	5. Question text here	1	0	0	0	4	100.00%	0.00%	0.00%
17	6. Question text here	0	1	0	0	3	0.00%	100.00%	0.00%
18	7. Question text here	0	0	1	0	2	0.00%	0.00%	100.00%
19	8. Question text here	0	1	0	0	3	0.00%	100.00%	0.00%
20	9. Question text here	1	0	0	0	4	100.00%	0.00%	0.00%
21	10. Question text here	0	0	0	1	1	0.00%	0.00%	0.00%
22	11. Question text here	0	1	0	0	3	0.00%	100.00%	0.00%
23	12. Question text here	0	0	1	0	2	0.00%	0.00%	100.00%
24	13. Question text here	0	1	0	0	3	0.00%	100.00%	0.00%
25	14. Question text here	1	0	0	0	4	100.00%	0.00%	0.00%
26	15. Question text here	0	1	0	0	3	0.00%	100.00%	0.00%
27	16. Question text here	0	0	1	0	2	0.00%	0.00%	100.00%
28	17. Question text here	0	0	0	1	1	0.00%	0.00%	0.00%

Survey Report / Survey Data

20 To print the Survey Report worksheet, click on the tab to make the worksheet appear on the screen. Place the cursor on File in the menu bar, click one time, scroll down to Print, then click once again. Click OK in the window that appears.

Extensions

Once you have customized the template and added data, you might also want to

- experiment with the Chart Wizard to graph the survey results

- copy and paste the Survey Report worksheet into a Word document for reporting purposes.

Standardized Test Scores

About This Template

A variety of grant applications and evaluation reports ask that standardized test scores for multiple years be reported by grade level in both chart and table formats.

Created in Excel, this template functions as a database that can be used to track annual standardized test scores by grade level. Once data are entered into the worksheet, the information can be sorted and filtered by grade level and year. In addition, the PivotTable and PivotChart Wizard feature can be used to generate tables and charts, which can then be taken into Word documents for reporting purposes.

SOFTWARE	Excel
ADDITIONAL EQUIPMENT	printer

Template View

Gr. Level	Year	Rdg. Comp.	Rdg. Voc.	Total Rdg.	Math Comp.	Math Prob. Solv.	Total Math	Language	Spelling	Science	Soc. Sci.

Directions

1 Open the template *Standardized Test Scores* (Standardized Test Scores.xls) found in the Briefcase Chapter 5 folder. (See Getting Started With the Templates in the introduction for directions on opening a template.)

2 The headings for columns C–L in row 1 coincide with the standardized test scores typically reported:

- Reading Comprehension
- Reading Vocabulary
- Total Reading
- Math Computation
- Math Problem Solving
- Total Math
- Language
- Spelling
- Science
- Social Science

These heading may be modified if needed.

To change a heading, place the cursor on the cell you wish to modify and click one time. Type the new heading and press Enter. Although the columns are shaded to assist in data entry and to visually cluster like test scores, the shading has no impact on the function of the worksheet.

If you modify the column headings, be sure to save the file before you proceed.

3 To enter data into the worksheet, place the cursor on a cell (A2 for the first entry) and click once. Type the grade level for the first set of scores.

4 Press the right arrow on the keyboard to move the cursor to cell B2. Type the year this set of scores represents, then press the right arrow to move to the next cell.

5 Continue entering information in this manner. If you do not administer a particular test at your site (e.g., science), leave the cell blank.

6 Repeat in subsequent rows as needed. See the sample below, which shows test scores for Grades 2–6 in Total Reading and Total Math for 2002 and 2003.

◇	A	B	C	D	E	F	G	H
1	Gr. Level	Year	Rdg. Comp.	Rdg. Voc.	Total Rdg.	Math Comp.	Math Prob. Solv.	Total Math
2	2	2002			45			54
3	3	2002			34			53
4	4	2002			23			22
5	5	2002			54			44
6	6	2002			32			64
7	2	2003			55			65
8	3	2003			33			44
9	4	2003			33			53
10	5	2003			22			44
11	6	2003			45			50
12								
13								
	◄ ◄ ► ►	Sheet1 / Sheet2 / Sheet3						

7 To save the file, click once on File in the menu bar, scroll down to Save As, and click one time. Type a name for the file that will make sense later (e.g., Standardized Test Scores 2002 and 2003), and click on the Save button.

MANIPULATING THE DATA

In addition to having grade-level scores for multiple years stored in one file, the value of this type of worksheet lies in the ability to manipulate data to generate reports and make quick comparisons.

Three data manipulation techniques are described below: sorting, filtering, and the PivotTable and PivotChart Wizard.

The sample above shows a worksheet that includes a few entries.

Sorting

8 Notice that while each grade level has scores entered for two years, the data is not in adjacent rows. To make a quick comparison of scores from one year to the next, place the cursor on cell A1 (Gr. Level) and click one time.

9 Click on the Sort Ascending button in the standard toolbar, or click on Data in the menu bar and select Sort, then click OK in the window that appears. The grade-level data are now displayed in adjacent rows, as shown below:

◇	A	B	C	D	E	F	G	H
1	Gr. Level	Year	Rdg. Comp.	Rdg. Voc.	Total Rdg.	Math Comp.	Math Prob. Solv.	Total Math
2	2	2002			45			54
3	2	2003			55			65
4	3	2002			34			53
5	3	2003			33			44
6	4	2002			23			22
7	4	2003			33			53
8	5	2002			54			44
9	5	2003			22			44
10	6	2002			32			64
11	6	2003			45			50
12								
13								
	◄ ◄ ► ►	Sheet1 / Sheet2 / Sheet3						

10 To sort numerically by grade level and by year, place the cursor on A1 and click one time. Click on Data in the menu bar and select Sort. A pop-up window appears. Because the cursor is in A1, the first sort will be by grade level. Click on the black arrowhead that appears next to the box under "Then by," click and scroll down to "Year," and click once again. The list is now sorted numerically, first by grade level, then year.

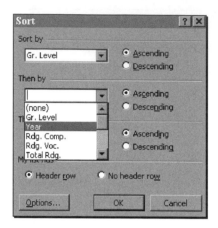

11 A sort of this type may be used in any column heading in row 1.

12 To print a sorted report, place the cursor on File, click one time, scroll down to Print, and click OK.

13 Unless new data were entered during the time the file was open, it is not necessary to save before closing.

Filtering

Filtering makes it possible to view only those entries that meet certain criteria, for example, those entries for Grade 3 test scores.

14 To use the AutoFilter feature, click on cell A1 and drag to highlight the row through cell L1.

15 Click on Data in the menu bar and scroll down to Filter. A pop-up menu appears. Select and click on AutoFilter.

16 Drop-down boxes with black arrowheads appear in cells A1 through L1. Click on the arrowhead displayed in cell A1. Read the choices given in the drop-down list, which includes all the different kinds of data in cells in column A. To view only Grade 3, scroll down to 3 and click one time.

17 To see all entries again, select Show All from the list.

18 You may filter the list setting criteria in any of the columns.

	A	B	C	D	E	
	Gr. Level ⇕	Year ⇕	Rdg. Comp ⇕	Rdg. Voc. ⇕	Total Rdg ⇕	Mat
1						
2	Sort Ascending	2002			45	
3	Sort Descending	2002			34	
4	✓ (Show All)	2002			23	
5	(Show Top 10...)	2002			54	
6	(Custom Filter...)	2002			32	
7	2	2003			55	
8	3	2003			33	
9	4	2003			33	
10	5	2003			22	
11	6	2003			45	
12						

Drop-down menu

19 To remove the AutoFilter, place the cursor on Data in the menu bar, click and scroll down to Filter. Select and click on AutoFilter in the pop-up menu that appears.

20 To print a filtered report, place the cursor on File, click one time, scroll down to Print, and click OK.

21 Unless new data were entered during the time the file was open, it is not necessary to save before closing.

PivotTable and PivotChart Wizard

To avoid creating a spreadsheet with 10 columns for every school year's test results, the worksheet is designed so that subsequent years' test scores are entered in rows, with the new year included in the data entry. This makes the worksheet more readable, but it can make using the Chart Wizard problematic when you want to compare scores at one or more grade levels from year to year. An easy solution is to use the PivotTable and PivotChart Wizard feature of Excel to generate this type of table or chart.

22 Place the cursor on cell A1, then click and drag to highlight the range of cells that include data you want to use. In the example above, cells A1 through H11 would be highlighted. It's not a problem if you highlight more data than you actually intend to use.

23 Place the cursor on Data in the menu bar, click one time, scroll down to PivotTable and PivotChart Report, and click once again. This activates the PivotTable and PivotChart Wizard.

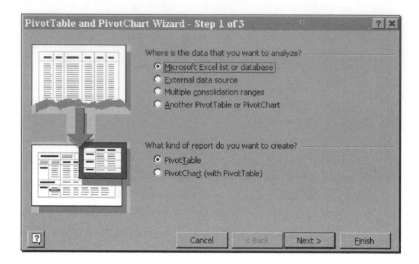

24 Accept the defaults on this first step to make a table. Click Next.

25 The data range was selected by highlighting cells before initiating the PivotTable and PivotChart Wizard. Click Next.

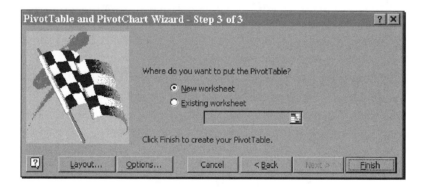

26 Click Next to place the PivotTable on a separate worksheet within the Standardized Test Scores file.

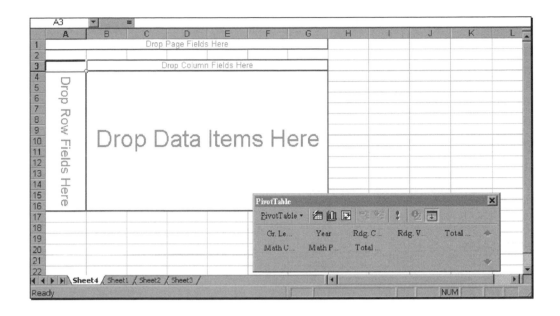

27 To create a table, click on a field name in the PivotTable window (in the red square) and drag it to one of the areas containing the word Drop. To create a PivotTable that compares 2002 and 2003 Total Math test scores in the sample given above, click and drag the field name Year into the area marked Drop Column Fields Here. Then click and drag the field name Gr. Level into the area marked Drop Row Fields Here. Finally, click and drag the field name Total Math into the area marked Drop Data Items Here.

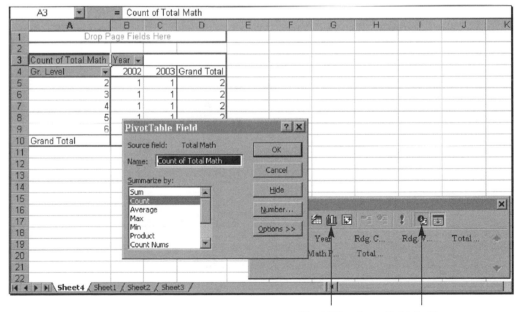

Chart Wizard   Field Settings

Notice that Excel immediately provides a count of the number of test scores reported for each grade level, but to compare the actual grade level score from one year to the next, it's necessary to tell Excel to display an average instead.

28 Click on the Field Settings button in the PivotTable toolbar (see above). Click on Average in the box headed "Summarize by." Then click on OK.

1	Drop Page Fields Here		
2			
3	Average of Total Math	Year ▼	
4	Gr. Level ▼	2002	2003	Grand Total
5	2	54	65	59.5
6	3	53	44	48.5
7	4	22	53	37.5
8	5	44	44	44
9	6	64		64
10	Grand Total	47.4	51.5	49.22222222
11			

29 The PivotTable now displays, by grade level, the Total Math scores for 2002 and 2003. It also gives an average score for the two years.

30 To chart the results of the PivotTable, click on the Chart Wizard button in the PivotTable toolbar (see above). The screen displays a chart with the 2002 and 2003 results in stacked columns (see below).

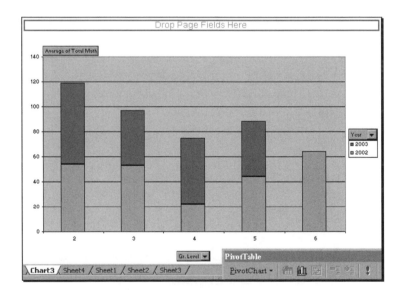

31 To place the 2002 and 2003 scores side by side, click the Chart Wizard button again.

32 Click on the first Chart sub-type in the first row of options.

33 Click on Finish. The information is now displayed in a chart showing side-by-side comparisons, by grade level, of test scores for two years.

34 To preserve the PivotTable and PivotChart, save the file again.

35 To print the PivotTable, click on worksheet tab Sheet 4, then place the cursor on File, click one time, scroll down to Print, and click OK.

36 To print the PivotChart, click on worksheet tab Chart 3, then place the cursor on File, click one time, scroll down to Print, and click OK.

PRINTING THE WORKSHEET

37 To print the original *Standardized Test Scores* worksheet, click on worksheet tab Sheet 1, then place the cursor on File in the menu bar, click one time, scroll down to Print, and click OK.

Extensions

Once you are familiar with the template, you may want to

- experiment with combining sorts and filters to generate very specific reports

- experiment with the Custom feature of AutoFilter to find specific score ranges

- experiment with additional PivotTables and PivotCharts.

Social, Legal, and Ethical Issues

CHAPTER SIX

VI. Social, Legal, and Ethical Issues

Educational leaders understand the social, legal, and ethical issues related to technology and model responsible decision making related to these issues. Educational leaders:

A ensure equity of access to technology resources that enable and empower all learners and educators.

B identify, communicate, model, and enforce social, legal, and ethical practices to promote responsible use of technology.

C promote and enforce privacy, security, and online safety related to the use of technology.

D promote and enforce environmentally safe and healthy practices in the use of technology.

E participate in the development of policies that clearly enforce copyright law and assign ownership of intellectual property developed with district resources.

The briefcase contains three word processing templates and three presentation template related to NETS·A VI. The chart below lists the templates included in this chapter and indicates the correlation between each template and one or more Standard VI performance indicators provided above. In this case, all five performance indicators are supported.

TEMPLATE	PROGRAM	NETS·A VI PERFORMANCE INDICATORS				
		VI.A.	VI.B.	VI.C.	VI.D.	VI.E.
Equal Access to Technology	Word	●				
Acceptable Use Policy Presentation	PowerPoint		●	●		
Online Safety Presentation	PowerPoint		●	●		
Checklist for K–12 School Web Sites	Word			●		
Ergonomics Survey	Word				●	
Copyright Policy Presentation	PowerPoint		●			●

Equal Access to Technology

About This Template

The Digital Divide encompasses far more than gender issues. Distribution of equipment, the kinds of activities students engage in, master schedules that permit college-bound students to enroll in technology electives, even the use of technology as a discipline technique must all be considered along with access provided to various academic student subgroups.

This template poses seven questions designed to assist in identifying areas of strength and weakness in a school's current approach to equity issues related to technology access. District-level leaders may wish to use this template with a group of principals, while site level leaders may choose to use it with a Leadership Team.

SOFTWARE	Word
ADDITIONAL EQUIPMENT	printer
	projection device (optional, to be used with a large group)

Template View

Equal Access to Technology: An Assessment Tool	
Site: School name here	**Completed by:** Your name here

Answer the following questions to identify areas of strength and weakness in your school's current approach to equity issues related to technology access.

	Yes	No
1. Are equal access issues addressed in your school site plan(s)?		
How?		

	Yes	No
2. Is access to technology used as a reward or punishment on your campus?		
How?		

3. Describe the age and location of computer equipment and peripherals on your site.

	Yes	No
4. Are students of all ages and academic ability levels offered equitable learning experiences in technology use?		
Describe typical learning experiences for grade levels and student subgroups.		

Directions

1 Open the template *Equal Access to Technology* (Equal Access to Technology.doc) found in the Briefcase Chapter 6 folder. (See Getting Started With the Templates in the introduction for directions on opening a template.)

2 Click on the first word in the text **School name here** to highlight the field, then type the school name. Press Tab to move to the next field.

3 Pressing Tab highlights the field. You may also double-click on the first word in the text **Your name here** to highlight the field, then type the name of the person completing the form. Do not press Enter.

4 Enter the answers to each question in the space provided by placing the cursor in the blank area and clicking once. A blinking vertical line will appear. This is the point at which text will appear as you begin to type the response to the question. Because this form is a table, the response area will expand if additional space is needed.

5 To save the file, click once on File in the menu bar, scroll down to Save As, and click once. Type a name for the file that will make sense later (e.g., Equal Access Assessment for 2003–04) and click on the Save button. The file will be saved in the Briefcase Chapter 6 folder on the hard drive. Remember to save the file frequently while you work, but do not rename it.

PRINTING THE FORM

6 To print the assessment form, click once on File in the menu bar, scroll down to Print, and click OK.

7 You may also print a blank form to use offline. To do this, complete Steps 1–3 and print the form before answering the questions. You may wish to do this when you want to work with a group to answer the questions and don't have computer access for all team members.

Extensions

Once you have answered the questions in the template, you might want to

- use either the Highlight or Font Color features on the formatting toolbar to emphasize key words and phrases in your responses to share with the Leadership Team, staff, and other stakeholders

- complete a form jointly if you have a projection device, asking individuals to answer the questions and having someone type the answers.

Acceptable Use Policy Presentation

About This Template

Acceptable Use Policies (AUPs) are a first line of defense for schools and districts when regulating staff and student use of the Internet on equipment and via services provided by the school district. However, to enforce an AUP, in addition to obtaining signatures of agreement from each staff member, student, and parent, it is important to hold an informational meeting in which the components of the AUP are explained.

Use this template to plan and present information about your school district's Acceptable Use Policy. General information about AUPs is provided, as are slides that may need to be modified to meet local conditions.

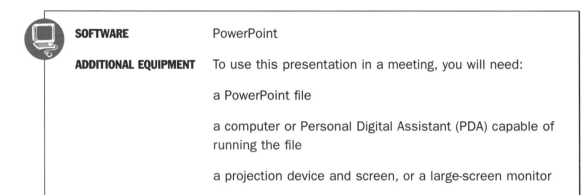

SOFTWARE	PowerPoint
ADDITIONAL EQUIPMENT	To use this presentation in a meeting, you will need:
	a PowerPoint file
	a computer or Personal Digital Assistant (PDA) capable of running the file
	a projection device and screen, or a large-screen monitor

Template View

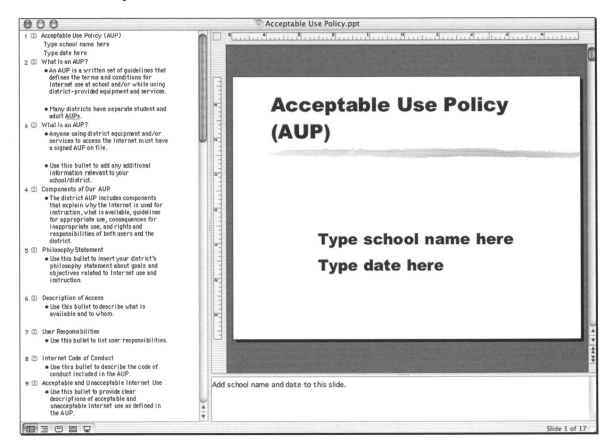

Directions

1 Open the *Acceptable Use Policy Presentation* template (Acceptable Use Policy Presentation.ppt) found in the Briefcase Chapter 6 folder. (See Getting Started With the Templates in the introduction for directions on opening a template.)

2 Click and drag across the text **Type school name here** to highlight the text, then type the name of your school. Do not press Enter.

3 Move the cursor down to click and drag across the text **Type date here**. With this text highlighted, type the date of the meeting. Do not press Enter.

4 Before proceeding, save the file. Click once on File in the menu bar, scroll down to Save As, and click once. Type a name for the file that will make sense later (e.g., Acceptable Use Policy Meeting 9-15-03), and click on the Save button. The file will be saved in the Briefcase Chapter 6 folder on the hard drive. Remember to save the file frequently as you work, but do not rename it.

CUSTOMIZING THE PRESENTATION

5 To move from slide to slide, either click on the scroll-down arrow on the right side of the window or click on the slide number in the outline pane. Using one of these methods, proceed to slide 2.

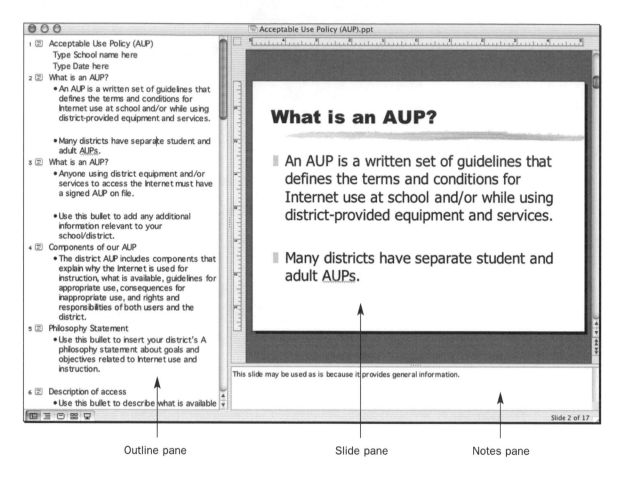

Outline pane   Slide pane   Notes pane

6 Look at the notes pane near the bottom of the window. In this template, the notes pane is used to provide suggestions for modifying slides. As the note suggests on this slide, it may be used as is.

7 Review slides 3–4. As noted, these slides may be used as is because they contain general information about Acceptable Use Policies. You may want to modify or add information to slides 3 or 4. To change a slide, click and drag across the text to be changed to highlight the text. Type the new text. If you do not need the additional bullet on slide 3, click and drag across the text to highlight it and press the Backspace key.

NOTE In customizing the slideshow, it may be necessary to delete an existing slide or add additional slides. For example, you want to combine onto one slide the district philosophy statement and description of access. In this case, change the heading on slide 5 to read Philosophy Statement and Access and add the bulleted statements. Then move to slide 6, place the cursor on Edit in the menu bar, click once, scroll down to Delete Slide, and click once again.

On the other hand, you may need multiple slides to describe access as outlined in your Acceptable Use Policy. In this instance, move to slide 6 and duplicate the slide by placing the cursor on Insert in the menu bar, clicking once, scrolling down to Duplicate slide, and clicking once again. Look at the outline pane to see two identical slides listed, one after the other. Move to the second slide, leave the title the same, and make necessary changes in the bulleted items.

8 Move to the slide titled Philosophy Statement. Highlight the existing bulleted text and add the district philosophy statement. If necessary, insert an additional slide.

9 Move to the slide titled Description of Access. On this slide, add a description of the kind of access offered by the district and to whom it is offered. To add an additional bullet, press Enter after a completed statement. If necessary, insert an additional slide.

10 Move to the slide titled User Responsibilities. Add a list of user responsibilities to this slide. To add an additional bullet, press Enter after a completed statement. If necessary, insert an additional slide.

11 Move to the slide titled Internet Code of Conduct. Add to this slide the main points of the code of conduct. To add an additional bullet, press Enter after a completed statement. If necessary, insert an additional slide.

12 Move to the slide titled Acceptable and Unacceptable Internet Use. Add examples of acceptable and unacceptable staff and student use of the Internet. To add an additional bullet, press Enter after a completed statement. If necessary, insert an additional slide.

13 Move to the slide titled Consequences for Inappropriate Use. Add a list of consequences to this slide. To add an additional bullet, press Enter after a completed statement. If necessary, insert an additional slide.

14 Move to the slide titled District Rights and Responsibilities. Add a list of rights and responsibilities to this slide. To add an additional bullet, press Enter after a completed statement. If necessary, insert an additional slide.

15 Move to the slide titled Additional Components of Our AUP. This slide lists typical additional components but may be modified as needed.

16 Move to the next two slides, titled AUP Enforcement. These slides list typical enforcement strategies but may be modified as needed.

17 Move to the two slides titled How Does This Impact Me? The items listed currently outline steps educators are generally asked to take in AUP enforcement. The slides may be used as is or modified to meet local needs. If using this presentation with students or parents, these items need to be modified. If necessary, insert an additional slide.

18 Move to the slide titled Questions? Add any specific resources or other information staff needs.

19 Save the file.

VIEWING THE PRESENTATION

20 To view the presentation, click on Slideshow in the menu bar, scroll down to View Show, and click once. The first slide (title slide) appears on the screen.

21 Use the right and left arrow keys to move back and forth through the slides.

Extensions

Once you have modified the information in this template for local use with staff, you might want to

- add clip art or pictures to enhance the presentation. Commands for doing this are found under Insert on the menu bar.

- modify the presentation for use with students or parents

- experiment with the various print options available:

  - the option Slides prints one slide per page

  - the option Handouts creates miniature versions of the slides on pages that participants can keep for later reference

  - the option Notes Pages prints the notes for each slide

  - the option Outline prints only the outline format for the presentation.

Online Safety Presentation

About This Template

The Children's Internet Protection Act (CIPA) of 2000 requires that districts receiving certain types of federal funds for technology purchases develop an Internet Safety Plan and hold community meetings to solicit input and keep parents informed about safety policies.

Use this template to plan and present a community meeting about online safety. General information about online safety and CIPA is included and may be used as is or modified to meet local needs. Places are provided to insert local information and strategies used to promote online safety in schools and at home.

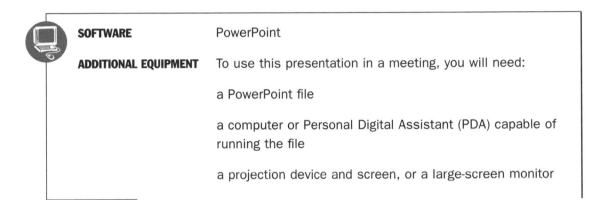

SOFTWARE	PowerPoint	
ADDITIONAL EQUIPMENT	To use this presentation in a meeting, you will need:	
	a PowerPoint file	
	a computer or Personal Digital Assistant (PDA) capable of running the file	
	a projection device and screen, or a large-screen monitor	

Template View

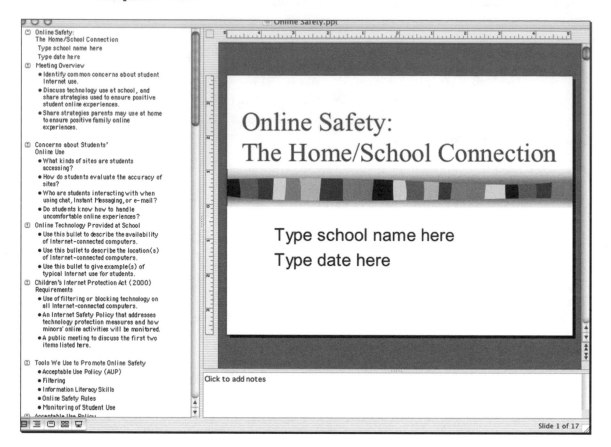

Directions

1 Open the *Online Safety Presentation* template (Online Safety Presentation.ppt) found in the Briefcase Chapter 6 folder. (See Getting Started With the Templates in the introduction for directions on opening a template.)

2 Click and drag across the text **Type school name here** to highlight the text, then type the name of your school. Do not press Enter.

3 Move the cursor down to click and drag across the text **Type date here**. With this text highlighted, type the date of the meeting. Do not press Enter.

4 Before proceeding, save the file. Click once on File in the menu bar, scroll down to Save As, and click once. Type a name for the file that will make sense later (e.g., Online Safety Meeting 9-30-03), and click on the Save button. The file will be saved in the Briefcase Chapter 6 folder on the hard drive. Remember to save the file frequently as you work, but do not rename it.

CUSTOMIZING THE PRESENTATION

5 To move from slide to slide, either click on the scroll-down arrow on the right side of the window or click on the slide number in the outline pane. Using one of these methods, proceed to slide 2.

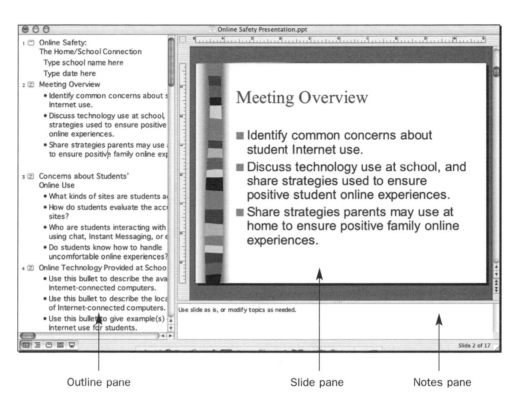

Outline pane   Slide pane   Notes pane

6 Look at the notes pane near the bottom of the window. In this template, the notes pane is used to provide suggestions for modifying slides. As the note suggests on this slide, it may be used as is or the topics may be modified to meet specific local needs. To change a slide, click and drag across the text to be changed to highlight the text, then type the new text.

7 Move to the slide titled Concerns About Students' Online Use. As noted, this slide may be used as is or modified to meet local needs.

8 Move to the slide titled Online Technology Provided at School. The bulleted text cues the information to enter for each item. Highlight each item, then type the information for your school.

NOTE In customizing the slideshow, it may be necessary to add additional slides. For example, describing the online technology currently at your site may require two slides. To duplicate the slide currently in use, place the cursor on Insert in the menu bar, click once, scroll down to Duplicate slide, and click once again. Look at the outline pane to see two identical slides listed, one after the other. Move to the second slide, leave the title the same, and make necessary changes in the bulleted items.

9 Move to the slide titled Children's Internet Protection Act (2000) Requirements. As noted, this slide should be used as is.

10 Move to the slide titled Tools We Use to Promote Online Safety. As noted, this slide may be used as is or modified to meet local needs.

11 Move to the slide titled Acceptable Use Policy. The bulleted text cues the information to enter for each item. Highlight each item and type the information for your school.

12 Move to the slide titled Filtering. The bulleted text cues the information to enter for each item. Highlight each item and type the information for your school.

13 Move to the slide titled 7 Steps to Developing Information Literacy Skills. As noted, this slide may be used as is or modified to meet local needs.

14 Move to the slide titled Online Safety Rules. List the specific online safety rules taught at your site. Click and drag to highlight the text for each bulleted item, and enter your own text.

15 Move to the slide titled Monitoring Use at School. List the specific strategies used at your site to monitor student online use. Click and drag to highlight the text for each bulleted item, and enter your own text.

16 Move to the slide titled The Home/School Connection. As noted, this transitional slide should be used as is.

17 Move to the slide titled Become an Active Participant in Your Child's Online Experience at Home. As noted, this slide may be used as is or modified to meet local needs.

18 Move to the slide titled Setting Rules for Online Use at Home. As noted, this slide may be used as is or modified to meet local needs.

19 Move to the slide titled Monitoring Use at Home. As noted, this slide may be used as is or modified to meet local needs.

20 Move to the slide titled Resources for Home. As noted, this slide may be used as is or additional resources may be added.

21 Move to the slide titled Questions? Add contact information.

22 Save the file.

VIEWING THE PRESENTATION

23 To view the presentation, click on Slideshow in the menu bar and scroll down to select View Show. Click once. The first slide (title slide) appears on the screen.

24 Use the right and left arrow keys to move back and forth through the slides.

Extensions

Once you have modified the information in this simple template for local use, you might want to

- add clip art or pictures to enhance the presentation. Commands for doing this are found under Insert on the menu bar.

- experiment with the various print options available:

  - the option Slides prints one slide per page

  - the option Handouts creates miniature versions of the slides on pages that participants can keep for later reference

  - the option Notes Pages prints the notes for each slide

  - the option Outline prints only the outline format for the presentation.

Checklist for K–12 School Web Sites

About This Template

School Web sites are often used as a vehicle to inform staff, students, and parents about Internet security and safety concerns. Sites should also provide safe and secure access to the Internet and provide models for staff and students that reflect positive use of the Internet as a communication tool (e.g., through the kinds of school and student information posted for public consumption).

Use this template to assess your school's Web site in relationship to Internet security and safety issues. Use it also to examine how well the Web site addresses the needs of various target audiences (staff, students, parents, and the community).

SOFTWARE	Word
ADDITIONAL EQUIPMENT	printer
	projection device (optional, to be used with a large group)

Template View

<table>
<tr><th colspan="3">Checklist for K–12 School Web Sites</th></tr>
<tr><td colspan="2">Site: School name here</td><td>Completed by: Your name here</td></tr>
<tr><td colspan="3">This checklist is designed to help school administrators assess the strengths and weaknesses of the school or district Web site, particularly as they relate to target audiences and Internet safety and security concerns.

Answer the following statements Yes or No. A No response may be a red flag for an issue you need to discuss with your Leadership Team.</td></tr>
<tr><td colspan="3" align="center">General Information</td></tr>
<tr><td></td><td align="center">Yes</td><td align="center">No</td></tr>
<tr><td>1. All students must have an up-to-date, signed Acceptable Use Policy on file before using school-provided technologies, including Internet access.</td><td></td><td></td></tr>
<tr><td>2. All staff members and parent volunteers must have an up-to-date, signed Acceptable Use Policy on file before using school-provided technologies, including Internet access.</td><td></td><td></td></tr>
<tr><td>3. The school or district Web site is used as the default Home page on-site.</td><td></td><td></td></tr>
<tr><td>4. The Web site is advertisement-free.</td><td></td><td></td></tr>
<tr><td>5. The district Acceptable Use Policy, Copyright Policy, and Internet Safety Plan are linked to the Web site.</td><td></td><td></td></tr>
<tr><td>6. Internet safety rules are posted on the Web site.</td><td></td><td></td></tr>
</table>

Directions

1 Open the template *Checklist for K–12 School Web Sites* (Checklist for K–12 Web Sites.doc) found in the Briefcase Chapter 6 folder. (See Getting Started With the Templates in the introduction for directions on opening a template.)

2 Double-click on the text **School name here** to highlight the field, then type the school name. Press Tab to move to the next field.

3 Pressing Tab highlights the field. You may also double-click on the first word in the text **Your name here** to highlight the field, then type the name of the person completing the form. Press Tab to move to the next field.

4 Each statement requires a Yes or No response. Mark the appropriate box by placing the cursor over the appropriate blank and clicking once. A blinking vertical line will appear, and you can type an X.

5 Space for comments is provided at the end of each section. Enter clarifying comments in the space provided by placing the cursor over the blank space and clicking once. A blinking vertical line will appear. Type comments. Because this form is a table, space for comments will expand if additional space is needed.

6 To save the file, click once on File in the menu bar, scroll down to Save As, and click once. Type a name for the file that will make sense later (e.g., Checklist for School Web Site for 2003–04) and click on the Save button. The file will be saved in the Briefcase Chapter 6 folder on the hard drive. Remember to save the file frequently while you work, but do not rename it.

PRINTING THE FORM

7 To print the checklist, click once on File in the menu bar, scroll down to Print, and click OK.

8 You may also print a blank form to use offline. To do this, complete steps 1–3 and print the form before responding to the statements. You may wish to do this when you want to ask Leadership Team members to answer the questions and don't have computer access for team members.

Extensions

Once you have answered the questions in the template, you might want to

- use either the Highlight or Font Color features on the formatting toolbar to emphasize areas marked No to discuss with the Leadership Team, staff, or other stakeholders

- modify the statements to reflect local needs or requirements by highlighting an existing statement and typing your own

- add statements by using the Insert Rows feature under Table on the menu bar

- complete a form jointly if you have a projection device, asking individuals to respond to the statements and having someone type the responses.

Ergonomics Survey

About This Template

The physical impact of long-term computer use by adults is well documented. Little has been done about collecting similar information concerning the physical effects on children; however, this is changing. A study was recently commissioned in New Jersey that will specifically examine ergonomics issues related to children's use of computers in schools. Administrators need to begin thinking about providing ergonomically sound workstations for both adults and children.

This template poses questions in three areas that are designed to assist you and your staff in identifying strengths and weaknesses in your school's current workstation environments for adults and students.

SOFTWARE	Word
ADDITIONAL EQUIPMENT	printer
	projection device (optional, to be used with a large group)

Template View

<table>
<tr><td colspan="3" align="center">Ergonomics Survey</td></tr>
<tr><td>Site: School name here</td><td colspan="2">Completed by: Your name here</td></tr>
<tr><td colspan="3">Use the following questions to identify areas of strength and weakness in your school's current approach to dealing with ergonomics concerns and technology use.</td></tr>
<tr><td></td><td>Yes</td><td>No</td></tr>
<tr><td>1. Does your technology plan address the issue of ergonomics as it relates to students and staff?
If so, how?</td><td></td><td></td></tr>
<tr><td>2. Visit locations where there are adult computer workstations. Which of the following accommodations are being made?</td><td>Yes</td><td>No</td></tr>
<tr><td>Keyboard trays are adjustable and at a negative slope to avoid wrist and arm strain.</td><td></td><td></td></tr>
<tr><td>The height and back support position of the workstation chair are adjustable.</td><td></td><td></td></tr>
<tr><td>The workstation chair has pivotable, adjustable armrests.</td><td></td><td></td></tr>
<tr><td>The mouse is placed on a tray or platform that can be positioned close to the body, above the keyboard.</td><td></td><td></td></tr>
<tr><td>The monitor is positioned so that the top is 2" to 3" above the user's line of sight.</td><td></td><td></td></tr>
<tr><td>The monitor is placed approximately one arm's length from the user.</td><td></td><td></td></tr>
<tr><td>The monitor screen is free from light glare.</td><td></td><td></td></tr>
<tr><td>Employees take frequent breaks when using the computer workstation (every 30–60 minutes.</td><td></td><td></td></tr>
<tr><td colspan="3">Based upon your observations, where do workstation modifications need to be made? What needs to be done?</td></tr>
<tr><td colspan="3">Less is known about the impact of long-term computer use on children. Because most students are not spending 3–4 hours daily using computers at school, it is likely that if injuries are sustained, they are happening at home. Schools can, however, intentionally</td></tr>
</table>

Directions

1 Open the template *Ergonomics Survey* (Ergonomics Survey.doc) found in the Briefcase Chapter 6 folder. (See Getting Started With the Templates in the introduction for directions on opening a template.)

2 Double-click on the first word in the text **School name here** to highlight the field, then type the school name. Press Tab to move to the next field.

3 Pressing Tab highlights the field. You may also double-click on the first word in the text **Your name here** to highlight the field, then type the name of the person completing the form. Press Tab to move to the next field.

4 Enter the answers to each question in the space provided by placing the cursor in the blank area and clicking once. A blinking short vertical line will appear. This is the point where words appear when you begin to type your response to the question. Because this form is a table, the response area will expand if additional space is needed.

5 To save the file, click once on File in the menu bar, scroll down to Save As, and click once. Type a name for the file that will make sense later (e.g., Ergonomics Survey for 2003–04), and click on the Save button. The file will be saved in the Briefcase Chapter 6 folder on the hard drive. Remember to save the file frequently while you work, but do not rename the file.

PRINTING THE FORM

6 To print the survey form, click once on File in the menu bar, scroll down to Print, and click OK.

7 You may also print a blank form to use offline. To do this, complete Steps 1–3 and print the form before answering the questions. You may wish to do this when you want to ask a group to answer the questions and don't have computer access for everyone.

Extensions

Once you have answered the questions in the template, you might want to

- use either the Highlight or Font Color features on the formatting toolbar to emphasize key words and phrases in your responses to share with the Leadership Team, staff, or other stakeholders

- complete a form jointly if you have a projection device, asking individuals to answer the questions and having someone type the answers.

Copyright Policy Presentation

About This Template

As technologies become increasingly sophisticated, it becomes easier for staff, students, and parents to inadvertently violate copyright law. This template is designed for use in a staff meeting to introduce basic information about copyright law and also to present information about the school district's copyright policy. It may be modified for use with older students and parents as well.

Use this template to plan and present information about your school district's copyright policy. General information about copyright, including public domain and fair use, is provided, as are slides that can be modified to meet local needs.

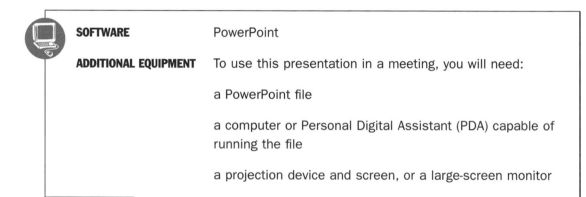

SOFTWARE	PowerPoint
ADDITIONAL EQUIPMENT	To use this presentation in a meeting, you will need:
	a PowerPoint file
	a computer or Personal Digital Assistant (PDA) capable of running the file
	a projection device and screen, or a large-screen monitor

Template View

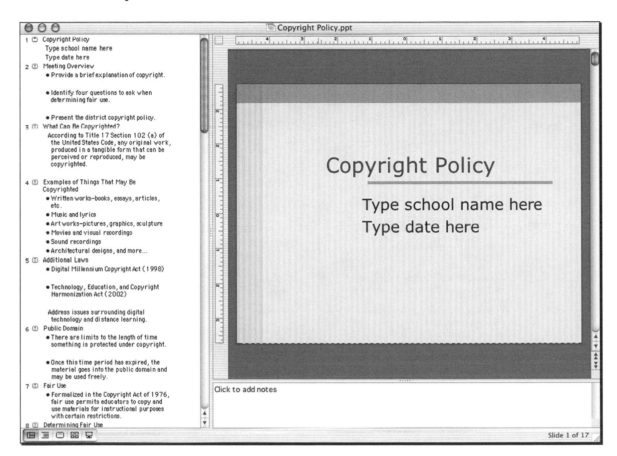

Directions

1 Open the *Copyright Policy Presentation* template (Copyright Policy Presentation.ppt) found in the Briefcase Chapter 6 folder. (See Getting Started With the Templates in the introduction for directions on opening a template.)

2 Click and drag across the text **Type school name here** to highlight the text, then type the name of your school. Do not press Enter.

3 Move the cursor down to click and drag across the text **Type date here**. With this text highlighted, type the date of the meeting. Do not press Enter.

4 Before proceeding, save the file. Click once on File in the menu bar, scroll down to Save As, and click once. Type a name for the file that will make sense later (e.g., Copyright Policy Meeting 10-1-03), and click on the Save button. The file will be saved in the Briefcase Chapter 6 folder on the hard drive. Remember to save the file frequently as you work, but do not rename it.

CUSTOMIZING THE PRESENTATION

5 As you move from slide to slide, either click on the scroll-down arrow on the right side of the window or click on the slide number in the outline pane. Use one of these methods to proceed to slide 2.

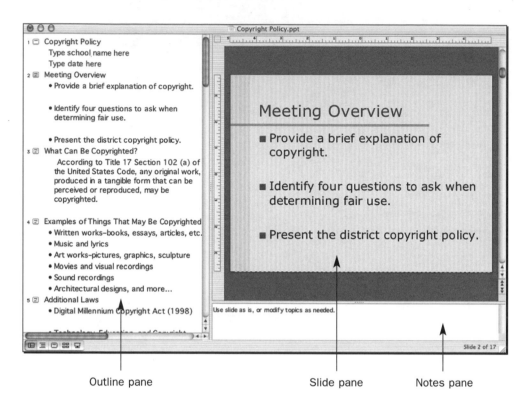

Outline pane   Slide pane   Notes pane

6 Look at the notes pane near the bottom of the window. In this template, the notes pane is used to provide suggestions for modifying slides. As the note suggests on this slide, it may be used as is or the topics may be modified to meet specific local needs. To change a slide, click and drag across the text to be changed to highlight the text, then type the new text.

7 Review slides 3–10. As noted, these slides may be used as is because they contain general information about copyright laws, public domain, and fair use.

8 Move to slide 11, titled District Copyright Policy. The bulleted text provides topics that should be covered in the copyright policy. However, to modify this list, highlight an item and type the information for your district's policy. Slide 12 provides space for additional topics that may be covered in your district's policy.